Structures
for the Church

David L E Berry

David + Rose

STRUCTURES FOR THE CHURCH

Reshaping the Christian mission
to our ancient western nations

David LE Berry

David L. E. Berry

Rose Castle 14th Feb: 2008

Gilead Books
Publishing
www.GileadBooks.com

First published in Great Britain, February 2008
by Gilead Books Publishing
Corner Farm
West Knapton
Malton
North Yorkshire YO17 8JB
www.GileadBooks.com

Cover illustration:
Mark 16:15 from the Novum Testamentum Graece by Nestle-Aland 2nd Edition, The German Bible Society. Used by permission. All rights reserved.
Jeremiah 7:4,8,23-24, 25b-26a, 27a; Mark 16:15a, 16:15b (RSV)
Jeremiah 7:22; Mark 16:15 (GNT)

Details for the Langeled pipeline courtesy of ukdeal.co.uk and 4.hydro.com/ormenlange
Details of the Sleipner gas field courtesy of statoilhydro.com

ACKNOWLEDGEMENTS

For over forty years my wife, Jennifer, has been on the receiving end of by far the longest stream of words about Church Structures. I owe her a big thank you for her enduring support.

For just under forty years I have been offering papers in pre-book form to friends, colleagues and members of the church hierarchy in the hope of honest confirmation where it was due and correction where it wasn't. My hope has not been disappointed. I now wish to record my thanks to the many people who have either made time to go through and comment on what I have written, or given various kinds of other help.

I would like to thank by name those who have encouraged and helped me more recently and more directly with this book:

Kate and Simon Ellis; Andrea and Richard Thompson; Bishop James Newcome; Jean le Guen; Sue Leathley; Robert Warren; Bishop Hewlett Thompson; Marion Wilcox; Tony Dent; Members of our local ecumenical prayer group; Nick Szkiler; Stephen Hazlett; Ruth Morrison; Jane Frenneaux; Sue Goodison; Rosemary James; Steve Axtell; Kendal Town Hall; Dr Crystal Davis; Chris and Lis Hayes.

Mapping produced with the assistance of Automobile Association Developments Limited 2008.

If I have missed anyone out I hope you will still accept my thanks.

David Berry

PREFACE

The germination of this book dates back to 1962 when, soon after reading law at university, I resumed my career as an accountancy student working in a City of London firm. To keep evenings free from household chores so I could do the accountancy correspondence course, I lived in a cheap hotel near Notting Hill Gate. I attended an Anglican church round the corner. It was lonely being 250 miles from my home in Cumbria. Yet, in loneliness terms, I was one of the lucky ones. Other students living in bed-sit land in the streets all around came from much further away, mostly Africa and the Caribbean.

My father's career had taken us as a family to an endless succession of new places. He had always instilled into his children the social value of the Church of England. Yes, the services were hard work to go to, but churchgoing was worth it. If in a new place you persevered at it, you eventually got to know new people. You weren't therefore lonely forever. After a while I did get noticed at that West London church, was eventually befriended, and found myself on the church council, aged 22.

However, I noticed that other students could not cope with a system that was so slow to welcome new faces. They generally lasted two Sundays and were never seen again. Their only chance of conversation seemed to be to reply "Good morning" to the vicar's "Good morning" as they shook his hand on the way out of church. On one occasion, as I took my turn to shake the vicar's hand behind a Nigerian student newcomer, I got very angry; I pushed my way out and ran down the street and across the Westbourne Grove traffic lights in order to catch him up and get to know him. In those days coffee after a service happened in college chaplains' rooms but had not yet reached parish churches. I decided it was time it should. At the next church council opportunity I announced that all we needed to do about evangelism was to dispose of half our pews nearest to the church door, and then serve coffee there after each Sunday service. They didn't get it. I soon realised why. It was because the whole parish system was mentally stuck in the ancient villages of England. The thinking went like this:

"Our village, North Kensington, had lost its squire some time ago but it still had its vicar. We could carry on with the pastoral system invented for the Middle Ages because everybody had been living, labouring, holy-daying and pub-visiting in the same little community for generations. Church was a religious duty within which there was no need to meet much face to face. You were doing that all day and every day anyway."

Here in front of my eyes was a blank refusal of the church even to consider the need to minister to people in "wholes", that is according to how they lived their lives as a group distinct from others (see Chapter 7, paragraph a). The church saw only parishioners; it was incapable of noticing the particular needs of one of the important wholes that lived in the neighbouring streets - poor Commonwealth students.

To one who had studied case law, the church showed a serious lack of reinterpretation of old principles in new situations. I could not sleep at night for wondering how such a system might be reconstructed to serve the gospel effectively in the 20th century. In the end, after a long struggle, I was persuaded that to be instrumental in helping such a system to change, I had to get right into it. Terrifyingly this involved ordination. It also meant working for some 33 years within a system with which I profoundly disagreed. I hope I have learnt something of value by having been at the coalface of parish ministry in five Church of England dioceses. If so, then some, at least, of what follows should ring true.

My visit to France as part of a two month sabbatical in 1996 was a major encouragement. I came across fellow Christians in three Catholic dioceses who had a profound grasp of the issues raised by outdated church structures. In two out of the three, my visit seemed to have been ordained to coincide with important initiatives to update the church's structure. For several days in the third, I was the guest of the priest who headed up the whole restructuring process for that diocese.

David Berry
Warcop
Cumbria
February 2008

CONTENTS

CONCLUSION   86

DIAGRAMS

INTRODUCTION

Christ's Great Commission

Christ sent his disciples into the world to preach the Kingdom of God. His great commission to them was to share the good news of his salvation with individuals, communities and nations. They were to do this in the fullest and most effective way possible. They were to be a body present and visible to the people in their everyday lives. They were to make a difference in society by the very fact of their presence. Jesus Christ referred to his followers being "salt" and "light" in the community around them. People are more receptive of a new message if they already have a positive experience of the wholesome influence and friendship of the people who bring that message. They best hear news when the news-bearer comes alongside them rather than shouting from a distance. When the church is close to society, it is more likely to speak in terms that are understood.

This book is about how, as disciples of Jesus, we can best be grouped so as to follow his instructions about being present within the communities we find in today's world. Put another way, I will examine how the church should organise its life to get as close as it can to the world Jesus sent it to.

Spreading the good news of Jesus does involve speaking the message to individuals, and individual conversion is vital if the Kingdom of God is to advance. But evangelism is also about reaching out to whole communities and finding the "key of the door" into them. Jesus taught his disciples this strategy in Matthew 10:11. Our job must include understanding whole communities within this world and infiltrating them with the aroma and word of Jesus Christ. If we neglect this, the corporate aspect of mission, we will fail in a large part of the task. On this point, a prophetic voice from across the Channel still needs to be heard loud and clear all over the church. We need the teaching of Canon Fernand Boulard, French writer on religious sociology in the mid 20th century. His book *Premiers Itinéraires en Sociologie Religieuse*[1] was translated in 1960 by Michael Jackson, later a Canon of Sheffield. The translation is entitled *An Introduction to Religious Sociology*[2]. What I have to offer in the chapters that follow may seem strange to the ears of some in our churches and be found quite hard to swallow, let alone digest. I am therefore grateful to be able to point to the work of such as Canon Boulard who laboured long before me on the subject of structure when looking into the church's failure. My references to Canon Boulard are all collected in Chapter 7 of this book.

The hard fact is that the historic western European church has not retained the mass of the population within recent times. Western Europe is the one part of the world where the church is failing to grow. Even where it is not shrinking statistically in Europe, it is for the most part losing the allegiance of the young. Why is this? Must we not at least take a hard look at the extraordinary weight of inherited church structure in Europe compared with other parts of the globe? Surely this great weight is at least part of what is crushing the missionary life out of our once Christian continent.

The church is no longer close to the world, in so far as its buildings and the stationing of its congregations have remained the same, while the world has developed into new shapes. The salt and light, which Jesus said we were to be in the world, are not reaching the places where they are needed. To a great extent the church has been left behind as God's creation has developed. This development, hastened on by the use of new technology, has produced big changes in the shape of our community life.

The problem facing much of the church in our ancient western nations is a chicken and egg one: too many church people lack a burning desire to reach out with the gospel to the nation around them; too many merely seek comfort in the organisation they regard as "their church". The way the church is set up encourages this attitude. Little wonder then such an organisation has remained the same while the way each of these nations is structured has changed. The author is indebted to Canon Robert PR Warren for pointing out what the outcome of a mere change of structure without a widespread change of outlook would be. Many existing church members would use a new structure as best they could to feather their own nests without regard to the church's mission. A change of heart is needed which feels the pain of our lack of mission to a lost generation. Resolve is needed to receive all that God provides to enable outreach with the gospel. This book about restructuring the church is offered in the first instance as an encouragement to us all to take note of how far we have fallen from the Early Church's missionary mind-set and to repent. The proposals I make are for very specific grassroots change. I believe they have to be written out in a blueprint style to stir the imagination of the majority who worship in our churches. I want to help as wide a Christian readership as possible to think mission. Mission should dictate the shape of the church; not the other way round.

Of course, we need the gospel ourselves before we can be interested in taking it to others. A spiritual breakthrough is needed in the western European church simply to get the gospel more fully received within many a congregation. Hearts and minds need setting free from looking inwards. As the Lord Jesus said, the greater blessing comes when we think about giving to others rather than just receiving. In the years since returning to England from my last Anglican appointment, I have been a member of an ecumenical prayer group. This has provided an opportunity to learn and take part in sustained prayer for the territory in which I have settled. The work consists of praying for the release of the land, its churches and its people, so that the gospel can be more clearly heard and received.

Once our hearts are right with God, not only on the subject of his mission to us, but also to other people, then thought and prayer can take place about the kind of church the Lord Jesus wants. The more Christians that get involved in such thinking and praying the better. The concrete proposals that I make for restructuring in this book, together with the reasons I give for them, need testing by prayer and waiting upon the Holy Spirit. Such testing is needed by those faithfully (and often wearily) involved in running the current structure of the denominations. It is also needed by Christian believers who live in the fast-lane of modern life and don't have time to sit on the councils of the churches. Often they are the very ones who see most clearly the current lifestyle of the nation; and for that reason they can grasp the more easily in what ways the church has become out of touch. By making specific concrete proposals I hope to help build the missionary vision of a wide cross-section in congregations. Changes that clear the way for mission will only happen if enough believers want them. If we are to have the new structures that we need, church leaders are going to need much vision, courage and dogged persistence, but their task will need complementing by vision, and a passion for the gospel, that wells up from the grassroots.

The aims of this book are:

- to show from the history of Christian mission how the western European church has been "left behind" (Chapter 1);

- to look afresh at some relevant New Testament teaching on mission and illustrate our failure to obey it with examples from everyday life (Chapter 2);

- to explore how society today is structured and identify the different overlapping communities in which we live our complicated lives (Chapter 2);

- to make proposals for restructuring the church so as to help it operate in the centre of today's communities (Chapters 2, 3 and 4). These proposals will only be specifically applied to Britain south (approximately) of the Scottish Border. They may, in principle, apply in other parts of Western Europe;

- to examine heritage issues and the challenge of change (Chapters 5 – 8).

The extent to which structures are outdated varies across the denominations

The church is most left behind where its structures are most ancient. Thus in England and Wales, where it has predominated for some hundreds of years, the Anglican church will be the main subject of study in Chapters 2 and 3. Nevertheless, all the historic churches need to have the best structure possible for coming alongside communities. In some instances non-Anglican denominations have structures that are relatively up-to date. For example the average rural Roman Catholic parish in England is likely to fit the reality of a smallish town and its satellite villages quite well. No doubt the reasons for this are to be found in the history of Roman Catholic expansion over the last 150 years. If we are willing under God to learn from history, then our past can be our teacher and friend, instead of our straitjacket.

Structure and Christian unity

The separateness of Christian denominations is not only based on specific differences of teaching and worship practice. It is also kept in place by the use of different structures. Working together is a lot easier for different denominations when their respective local structures are already similar and also relate to the structure of the area. Where the Anglican, Roman Catholic and Free Church authorities have each seen fit to let a particular area be operated as a single pastoral unit, at least the churches will benefit from their clergy being similarly stationed and therefore more likely to find time in their diaries to meet regularly. It is much harder to do this when pastoral units are dissimilar and there are more clergy of other denominations to try to keep in contact with whose work is only partly over the same patch of ground. There are likely to be geographical reasons when similarity of the pastoral unit occurs especially if the unit also fits the shape of the local community. The geography in such instances may well be that the place is an "island" of at least 10,000 population surrounded by either seawater or thinly populated countryside.

Denominations best meet the challenge of change when they do mission together

When a decision is made to work together, different denominations are more likely to adjust their own shape to the needs and shape of the area to be served. Co-operation between denominations has the effect of loosening the grip of congregations on their inherited structure. This is true both from a spiritual point of view and a legal one. Many a local church, left to its own devices, will insist on keeping inherited structures regardless of their usefulness in present-day mission. Inter-church and interdenominational mission can act as a lever to overcome this problem. When eyes are refocused on co-operation with other Christians they are more likely to be also focused on co-operation with Jesus Christ.[3]

The Anglican Church south of the Scottish border has an appalling record of clinging to outdated structures. Without the lever of binding agreement to co-operate with other denominations, this Anglican structural inertia is likely to remain intact until much of the Anglican structural tradition dies a natural death. To save Anglican insights into Christian truth for the benefit of future generations in the UK as a whole, we need the help of other denominations to release Anglicans from the shackles of the past.

CHAPTER 1   REVIEW OF OUR CHRISTIAN MISSION OVER 20 CENTURIES

Before trying to work out what structures would serve to bring the church more fully among the peoples of modern Western Europe, we need to learn all we can from the experience of the past. There are two tasks here: the first is to learn from that distant age in our continent's history at what stage the church first found itself with outdated structures and proceeded to do something about it; the second task is to learn about the next occasion when the church found itself with outdated structures and to admit that some 250 years later it has still only tinkered about with the problem.

The church from New Testament times until the collapse of Roman civilisation (the period of the Roman Empire)

As we follow the story in Acts of how the Early Church carried out Christ's commission from the Day of Pentecost onwards, we find that new churches were formed in each of the cities of the Roman Empire. Acts traces the progress of the gospel from Jerusalem to Rome via such places as Antioch, Ephesus and Malta. St Paul is a key figure in this.[4] By the second century the church in a typical city had a bishop permanently in charge who was assisted by elders. Roman cities had good public facilities that had been modelled on those used by the ancient Greeks for their cities. These very civilised communities were well linked to each other by a road network the length and breadth of the Empire. They were easily accessible from their neighbouring countryside. The city bishopric remained the normal way for the church to be amongst the bulk of the people for as long as the Roman Empire was the major power in Europe.

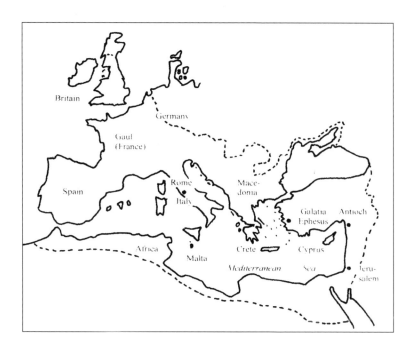

Diagram 1   THE ROMAN EMPIRE IN THE SECOND CENTURY AD[5]

When church buildings were constructed in the fourth century they were modelled on law courts/city halls and so took the name "basilica". The more remote countryside was largely unevangelised, and our word "pagan" comes from the Roman word for countrymen – "pagani".

Diagram 2   PUBLIC BUILDINGS AND FACILITIES IN A ROMAN CITY CENTRE
1   Pedestrian crossing   2   Horse drinking trough   3   Stadium   4   Temple   5   Law courts

The Dark Ages

When the western half of the Roman Empire started to crumble after AD 400, civilisation in our part of Europe underwent a big change. As wave after wave of invaders swept in from the North and East, the "Dark Ages" eventually brought an end to the Graeco-Roman city community. After the Roman armies pulled out in AD 410, Britain was invaded for the next 650 years successively by Angles, Saxons, Jutes, Danes, Norsemen and Normans.

Diagrams 3.1 & 3.2 HOW IT FELT TO BE INVADED – A BRITISH ESTUARY IN ABOUT AD 800

In this illustration the warrior's helmet has been given horns. This is to indicate how the settled and largely Christian population might have felt in the face of the Nordic threat. A type of helmet more likely to have been worn by the invader in the picture is shown on the next page.

After 410 the old Roman cities did not thrive under the onslaught of the invasions. They were too easily found by newly arrived invaders who simply followed the main roads. The population took to the countryside and found refuge in small and isolated farming communities. As time went on these rural communities became rigidly built into a class system. This was designed to provide for the defence of the kingdom that had taken over in that particular part of the former empire.

In England it even became the law that the mass of farm workers were not allowed to move from their villages without the permission of the lord of the manor. Bishops based in the old cities found they could no longer pastor their scattered and static flocks. They therefore sent out elders to take permanent charge of small rural congregations.

1   Communal living
      quarters in a
      chieftains hall

2   Palisade and ditch

3   Stream

4   Edge of the forest

Persons:

  In foreground
  Swineherd

  In background
  Cowherds

Diagram 4   ANGLO-SAXON SETTLEMENT - AD 650

The picture below shows an inland canal connecting at high tide to a wharf on a tidal river.

Diagram 6   UK INDUSTRIAL LANDSCAPE – AD 1820

This canal passes under a road in the middle distance and then proceeds into the industrial area in the distance. As shown by the bottle kilns, much of the industry is china production for which there would have been a need for the bulk transport of coal and china clay if these were not available from nearby mines and pits.

By the beginning of the 20th century there had been further change: the more affluent could now commute to and from work by rail transport.

Diagram 7   THE AGE OF STEAM – AD 1920

In the latter part of the 20th century and into the present day, transport has developed to such a degree that a large proportion of the population currently travel long distances to work each day. Living in one place and working in another has changed the shape of society even more significantly. Long-distance travel for leisure, even for a few hours, has further altered the pattern of relationships in a given area.

Diagram 8   MOTORWAY SEEN FROM A CAR – AD 2000+

Note: the motorway signpost is visible in good time for high speeds. It also points to a whole region.

With the arrival of all this change in the way people live and form their community life, the ancient churches of Western Europe have largely tried to cling to the rural-style parish. They have disobeyed the Lord's precise instructions in the Gospel of Mark[6] about being set in the midst of society. One great and prophetic figure who stood against this disobedience was John Wesley. He was an 18th century Anglican priest who saw that the UK parish system was not reaching the new industrial communities. Opposed by the disobedient rural-style parish system, he was determined to fulfil his calling as an evangelist. On one occasion in 1739 he had a frank exchange with Bishop Butler of Bristol, who objected to his open air preaching to mineworkers in his diocese. In that year John Wesley declared, "I look upon all the world as my parish"[7].

Wesley proceeded to minister the gospel to the new communities, whether or not he was welcome within the local Anglican parish. His ministry was eventually rejected by the Anglican establishment and the Methodists had no option but to form a separate denomination. More than two centuries later we have still not taken his words to heart. We are still struggling to maintain the parish system even if only in terms of its historic buildings.

CHAPTER 2   MISSION TO ALL THE MODERN WORLD?

A –"Go into all the world and preach the gospel to the whole creation" (RSV)

Christ's comprehensive commission to us

This verse, Mark 16:15, is not part of the original version of Mark's Gospel. It does however convey to us a true New Testament component of Christ's commission to his disciples to take the gospel to the world.

The original Greek[8] for this commandment to the disciples is phrased to emphasise how comprehensive Christ's commission is. In the equivalent text in Matthew 28:19 we simply find the expression "all nations" (RSV) (that is, the disciples, who are all Jews, are commanded to take the gospel to the Gentiles). Here in Mark there is a greater focus on human life as God has created it on earth. The church here is being sent to the whole created order of human beings.[9] This verse from the ending of Mark's Gospel seems to have a message for us: we no longer have a problem over the great gulf between Jews and Gentiles, but do have one over another kind of gulf. This is the one that has opened up between the historic mission of the church and the newly created shape of modern life.

Our failure to obey with three examples

As mentioned in the introduction, Christ had in his earlier teaching already taught about his followers being salt and light for the world. His parable of the yeast, which is also about the spread of his gospel life in the world, is especially apt for our present predicament. We have failed to take a piece of old dough saved from the last baking and plant it in the midst of the new dough which stands for the new "lump" or framework of human life which has come into being since that last baking. Our failure consists of our having clung to the village-style parish as our way of going with the gospel to the whole creation. We are doing this in the mistaken belief that where people's homes are found is where their life is lived virtually all the time. Unfortunately for the church in this situation, large parts of people's time are now spent a long distance from their homes.

If men, women and children are working, learning and having leisure in places far away from their home neighbourhood, then there is bound to be a loss of opportunity to witness to the population today compared with what there would have been in the settled rural period of AD 750-1750.

We can take three examples in which we can see (1) how widely spread is the new framework of our western lifestyle, and (2) the church's structure problem and consequent failure to go with the gospel.

- From the world of leisure:

A Manchester or Lyon (South East France) family spends every other weekend rock climbing in mountains 100 miles away. The church is present in those mountains through a number of village parish churches. Each of these says something like this: "We are an ancient Christian shrine and an important attraction on your tourist route. For the church key apply to the farmhouse across the road. Our Sunday service is at 10.30 am."

The church's structure problem
The rock-climbing family may want to reach the rocks by first light, or at least have a reasonable place in the climbing queue. Instead of a 10.30am service they would be much more attracted to a short open air meeting at 6.00am in the car park further up the valley. The hard-pressed minister and local Christian leadership are struggling to maintain a portfolio of church services for small year-round mountain communities. Such specialist outreach to groups of rock climbers is beyond their capacity; they have few means of keeping in touch with rock climbers who just appear by car from miles away. The headquarters of rock-climbing organisations may not even be local but in a distant city.

- From the world of rural young people

The children in a lowland rural area go to primary school in the village where they live. Their parents are employed in towns and cities between six and sixty miles away, in one or two rural trades and to a small extent in agriculture. On going to secondary school at eleven in the nearest market town, many of the children become used to ranging across both that town and its surrounding countryside. This is because of their leisure interests and school friendships. The church in their home village is alongside only a small part of the world they now live in: the scale of its celebrations will rarely match that of school functions or of the town with which they are now familiar. The activities of their village church will be seen as boring.

The church's structure problem
Even supposing that in the area served by the market town the churches combine to operate a Christian youth outreach, what will become of the teenage converts resulting from this effort? If they want to belong to the church "properly" they will have to go their separate ways back to their parish churches as virtual loners. Otherwise they must simply remain in a loose federation relying on the next major Christian youth event in the area for spiritual encouragement.

- From the world of towns

Residents of a block of 19th century terraced housing in a large industrial town have in their midst a 900-seater church. It is located in a quiet street. As in many English country villages this 900-seater has a church primary school alongside it. Apart from the school, all centres of community such as sub-post office, take-away, off-licence etc, are some distance away from the church. The residents are nearly all highly mobile.

They see the church building as just as convenient, should they need it for a funeral or wedding, as any of the dozen similar buildings across the town.

The church's structure problem

The church's heavy investment in this type of building is not merited by the meagre results. There is frustration for those Christians who do struggle to keep it going because they have little energy left to spread the Word of God. Any threat of closure tends to produce an even greater burden in the short term. Faithful believers then find they are faced with apathy turned to militant nostalgia. Nostalgia will also often be a distinctive problem within such a church. It is likely to contain people who originated in this part of town but have become successful enough to move out to wealthier areas in the suburbs, yet commute back on Sundays to "keep the old church going". Unfortunately their witness to the gospel is not sufficiently tested in the district around the church between Monday and Saturday. Such churches are frequently afflicted by the evils of power seeking and party spirit.

In each of the above examples, the church is continuing to pour its major resources into being present in the type of area where the whole shape and framework of the human order no longer operate.[10] The energies of Christians are being significantly misdirected, and they are being hindered from going into all the world. Being unsuccessful in spreading the gospel, the few workers in each of these three types of church are likely to find that "running the church" demands a disproportionate amount of their time. In many cases they will lack space in their lives to deepen their relationship with the Lord Jesus, with their families, or to befriend unbelievers. The ghetto they form is not attractive to outsiders.

In these three examples we see that the church has failed to do what it did in the Dark Ages, that is to remodel itself to fit, and be alongside, the new reality of community life. Thus the church has failed to obey Christ's commission and has allowed a great gulf to arise between itself and the community at large.

Exceptions to such failure have been insufficient in extent to alter materially the general picture of misdirected energy. These exceptions at least show that the church did over recent centuries perceive that the parish couldn't quite do everything. UK examples of such exceptions are: ministries performed in the Armed Forces; the East India Company; hospitals and colleges. Since the Second World War there has at last also been recognition by the churches of the physical separation of large industry from the home life of people. Industrial chaplaincy has been set up on a modest scale. There is the Industrial Mission Association which co-ordinates training and review nationally. In some areas of the country the work is strong; in others it is virtually non-existent. Sadly, the pressure to maintain the parish system has been allowed to squeeze Church of England's contribution. Industrial mission needs to grow, not necessarily through the stationing of a greater army of full-time industrial chaplains, but rather through the continued increase in numbers of trained associate chaplains, both lay and ordained. Anglican parishes tend to be greedy for a minister's time, so proper arrangements need to be in place to safeguard industrial mission if it is done by a vicar part-time. Industrial mission needs affirming by the whole body of the church, which itself needs to be re-ordered to be in a position to do this.[11]

This same failure highlighted in Scotland

The gulf between the church as an institution and the new shape of human life is referred to in a report to the General Assembly of the Church of Scotland in 2001 entitled *Church Without Walls.*[12] In a section on page 11 dealing with the purpose of the church as written down for its constitution in the Articles of 1921, this report quotes the Third Declaratory Article:

> "As a National Church, representative of the Christian Faith of the Scottish people, it acknowledges its distinctive call and duty to bring the ordinances of religion to the people in every parish of Scotland through a territorial ministry."

The report then points out the need now at the beginning of the 21st century to question the assumptions behind this statement of purpose. This is because church and society have changed. Six assumptions are then tackled one by one. Dealing with the fourth assumption on page 12, the report describes it thus:

> "The 'territorial ministry' is taken as a norm, assuming social stability and cohesion. Today we recognise the many sector ministries that have emerged in the past 50 years in industry, hospitals, universities, technology and the arts."

It then proceeds to explain why it is incorrect and what should be the church's approach:

> "Society is such that everybody lives in a parish, but nobody lives in a parish. People belong to networks of friendship, work and leisure pursuits, or associate with the 'flow cultures' of transient groups of people. Apart from rural communities, the virtual community of the docu-soaps or the internet may be more real than the neighbour next door."

> "The future lies in sharing partnerships with neighbouring congregations of various traditions, and tapping into sector specialisms designed to connect with people in their work, leisure or crisis moments."

On page 13 the report sets out points made by Professor Steve Bruce, sociologist of Aberdeen University:

> "… the core issue is the erosion of belief: the lack of plausibility of faith for many people. This has undermined the confidence of many Christian people and made communication more complex as we have become immersed in the televisual culture. The social basis of the church has become disconnected from local community, through social fragmentation and congregational isolation."

And on page 14:

> "Shifts in population, informal patterns of relating, and interactive styles of communication mean that the physical buildings are often the wrong size, in the wrong style or in the wrong place. The General Trustees estimate that the Church of Scotland needs only 1,700 of its current 2,500 buildings."

Also on page 14, by way of sub-section heading, the report quotes Jeremiah 1:10, and asks a tough question:

> "'Destroy and overthrow' (RSV): What areas of church life are to be actively demolished?"

It then proceeds to answer this question by insisting that the 19th century norm for missionary strategy must be replaced by a 21st century one:

> "The Church of Scotland mission strategy is based on the 19th century mission model: one minister in one building in one parish. All the resources of the uniting church of 1929 were harnessed to servicing this strategy.

> "As we enter the 21st century, the emerging pattern for mission strategy must be much more diverse to permeate the fragmented nature of our society: ministry teams operating in a variety of community bases to be incarnate in a network of communities. Instead of occasional variations to the assumed 19th century norm, it is time to recognise the new components of the new strategy and resource it accordingly.

> "As we enter the 21st century we believe the shape of the church needs to be turned upside down...."

The authors of this Scottish report are clearly grasping the nettle of the church institution being left behind by developing creation and thus becoming unviable. Their point that society is now fragmented needs putting in context and qualifying. From the standpoint of the parish, society certainly has fragmented, but in other senses it has come together in a way undreamed of by our ancestors of one or two centuries ago. It is now possible to be in close and instant touch with people on the other side of the world both as individuals and as nations. It is also possible to travel for work, rescue and leisure on a scale and at a speed never imagined by our ancestors. In the light of global warming Christians should not be addicted to travel for its own sake but rather be full of quiet confidence and stillness in the Lord. They should be foremost in practising good stewardship of the planet and its resources. Technology, including the ability to travel fast, is part of God's creation. Rightly used, it should be welcomed and responded to by the church rather than deplored as the reason behind fragmentation. God's people should continue to go into his creation with his Holy Word – whatever shape that creation turns into.

Going into the "whole creation" of human life today

How should we obey the full meaning of Mark 16:15 for today? By way of a specific study, in what fashion should we do this in England and Wales? We need answers here to three questions:

- What currently, rather than historically, is the typical area in which a family lives and functions for the full range of its regular activities? What is its "life zone"?[13]

- What overlapping communities go to make up that typical life zone?

- How can the church be structured so as to be fully present in Britain south of the Scottish border?

During the period of the Roman Empire the place where most people lived out their weekly routine was the city. This was their life zone. After the collapse of the Roman Empire, it was the village or small rural town that formed the life zone for the majority of the population. Following the industrial developments of the 18th and 19th centuries clusters of towns began to sprawl across the landscape. These then became most people's life zone. These urban sprawls were connected first by canals, then railways, then trunk roads.

From the 20th century onwards, commuting for work, education, leisure and other services has, as explained above, produced a totally new framework of human living. God's creation has moved on. The most significant change has been that already mentioned: the separation of a person's home life and work life by what are often long distances. For this reason the Scottish *Church without Walls* report is so right to have printed that wonderfully meaningful sentence:

"Society is such that everybody lives in a parish, but nobody lives in a parish."

How families now live in regions

Everybody is resident in a parish, but where they wholly live – their life zone – is not a parish. The modern life zone has become so much bigger, not only because of the distance between many people's home and work life, but also because services to people have become highly specialised. Education, health, commercial and leisure services, and products of a very great variety and sophistication, are now offered to the consumer. People will happily travel to get exactly what they require. Therefore the life zone now consists of a region roughly 100 miles across. The way television organises itself to express the life of communities is clear evidence of this. Another obvious pointer is the motorway system: 19th century roads linked towns; motorways now link regions. To do this they have to ring the bigger communities that would otherwise obstruct through-traffic.

Britain is a relatively narrow land mass. Regions have in many cases come into being around and across major estuaries. This is because estuaries have enabled industry to prosper. They have provided good import-export facilities and flat land to easily accommodate large manufacturing plants. Estuaries, which were once major frontiers for places like Northumbria and South Wales, now form the centre of life zones. See maps (with approximate life zone boundaries) below:

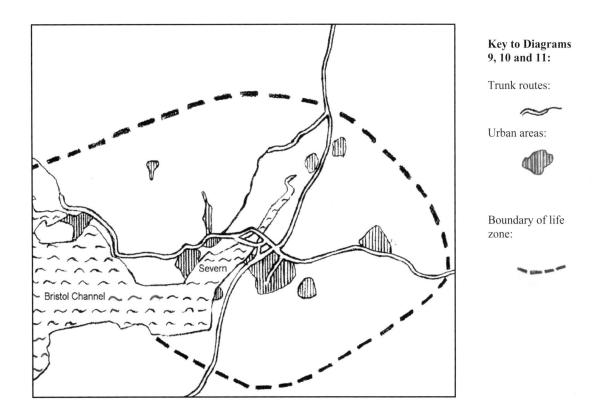

Key to Diagrams 9, 10 and 11:

Trunk routes:

Urban areas:

Boundary of life zone:

Diagram 9   LIFE ZONE BASED AROUND THE SEVERN ESTUARY

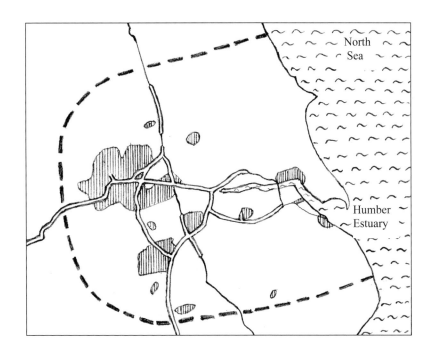

Diagram 10   LIFE ZONE LINKED TO THE HUMBER ESTUARY

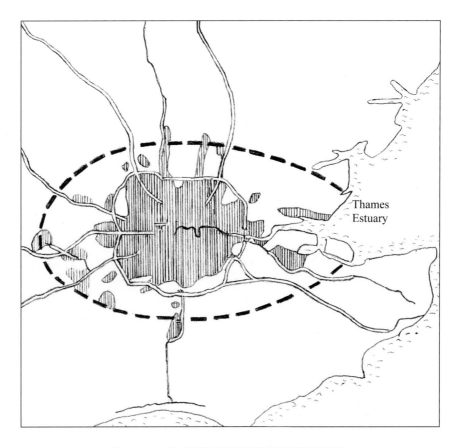

Thames
Estuary

Diagram 11   THE THAMES LIFE ZONE

Note: As there have been river bridges in London for nearly 2000 years this life zone's ancestry is longer than most.

In each of these diagrams the scale of the territory in which people live and work on a daily basis is reflected by the layout of the motorway system.

The overlapping communities that go to make up a typical region (= a life zone)

Here "region" will be used to mean an area similar in size but different from a government region.

In British regions there are usually distinctive key industries which are big enough to affect the life of the whole region. We have already mentioned estuaries as the hubs of regions because they provide facilities for worldwide trade and heavy industry. Other types of distinctive key industry which can define a region are large-scale food production on best quality land, tourism, and good international communications. An existing large area of towns, which attracts new industries because of its market size, also has the effect of forming a region.

Within Britain the boundaries of local government areas are different from those of the life zone region. Nevertheless, in terms of the daily life of ordinary people, these regions are indeed the zones into which families move and in which they set up their homes. If a national business sends one its employees to a new post in another part of Britain, that

32

person may well look around at the advantages and disadvantages of living in a number of different places. A home only 13 miles from the regional office or depot in a rather stressful urban environment may be compared with the advantages and disadvantages of living in rural peace 43 miles from this office or depot. A further consideration may well be the number of days per month that the firm will be requiring the worker to be at this regional centre rather than in other parts of the region. In nearly all cases, the place where a person or family sets up home remains the biggest part of their belonging to a given region. Yet there are many other parts of a region which are likely to contribute to the rich tapestry of a family's social life. These could be places where different family members work, receive specialist health care or higher education, go for sport or leisure activities or the administration of justice. Such a range of services is usually not available in any one local government area.

The church structured so as to be fully present region by region

Working out, first in theory and then in practice on the ground, how the church should be present in a life zone with a physical diameter of around 100 miles is bound to be a complicated business. To do this today is much more complicated than the task which faced the bishops at the end of the Dark Ages. They found the right form of mission to reach the new shape of society. We are faced with an equivalent task. Just because something is complicated is not a reason for not doing it, especially when Jesus in his gospel has specifically commanded that we do it. His commission to the Apostles included leading and guiding the church into the whole current created order of human society. For those who at present are in positions of oversight and leadership this may appear a near impossible task. In the case of the Church of England there is a built-in system for resisting even quite small pastoral change.

The next chapter will explain further a plan for twelve church provinces as shown on page 35. These provinces are substantially the twelve regions, or life zones, in which people now actually live out their daily lives in and around England and Wales. This chapter will provide a number of comparisons. These will be between the proposed church provinces and the current structures of a cross-section of UK churches, motorway and television networks, and the government regions. The motorway and television comparisons will highlight how real these proposed life zone provinces are in people's lives. The chapter will also show how such fresh provinces would support the identity and economic aspirations of each region.[14]

The author, being Anglican, is at ease with an episcopal structure within the church, ie archbishops and bishops, and it will be seen that these offices have been freely incorporated in the proposed plan of twelve provinces. However this book is in no way about the merits or demerits of episcopacy. It is about reshaping the mission of the whole church to fit current social conditions. There is no desire to exclude churches which operate without these traditional forms of leadership ministry. Those denominations that do not use these categories still have ordained people in positions of pastoral oversight and/or general secretaryship. Non-episcopal terminology includes chairman, president etc. The author would wish those who read this book who are not in episcopal churches to mentally substitute other terminology as they follow through the argument for radical change.

Obedience is usually costly but with God's help always possible. Obedience to Mark 16:15 is certainly costly to much of the church's present outlook and structure. What is proposed is a leap for any of our current denominations. Some denominations would find the leap was greater for them than for others. Would that the mass of British Christians were ready take a leap of faith for the Kingdom of God. The problem we face at the moment is firstly of being "just about able to manage as we are", and secondly that "anyway, if we were to change our system the way we get the money in would be lost and we wouldn't be able to pay our clergy". Perhaps that problem is about to be solved by the losses of congregation and income if we continue to struggle to maintain so much traditional and obsolete structure for a nation that has shut its ears to the Bible. A leap of faith by a number of denominations into a shared structure has already been done on a small scale in places where there is an LEP (Local Ecumenical Programme). We just need to do it nationally. There awaits a great prize – that of spiritual unity.

In Chapter 8 I will put forward some suggestions for the way forward into obedience. A new set of church provinces as illustrated on the opposite page could, for some, cut costs. In the Anglican situation, if we include the Diocese in Europe, there are 50 diocesan offices for England and Wales. Forty-nine of these are all busy dealing with the organisational needs of an area where travel to them for meetings is not always more convenient than it would be if 12 better placed centres were used.

For many Christians now working hard to maintain the local structures of their church at whatever level, the following map may appear a real launch into the deep. Yet in much of our land that local structure is a burden that squeezes gospel work off the church's agenda. In the long term we cannot afford outdated structures. For a few years yet they will no doubt continue to feel like a comfort zone for some, but there is no escaping the fact that they eat up precious Christian resources.

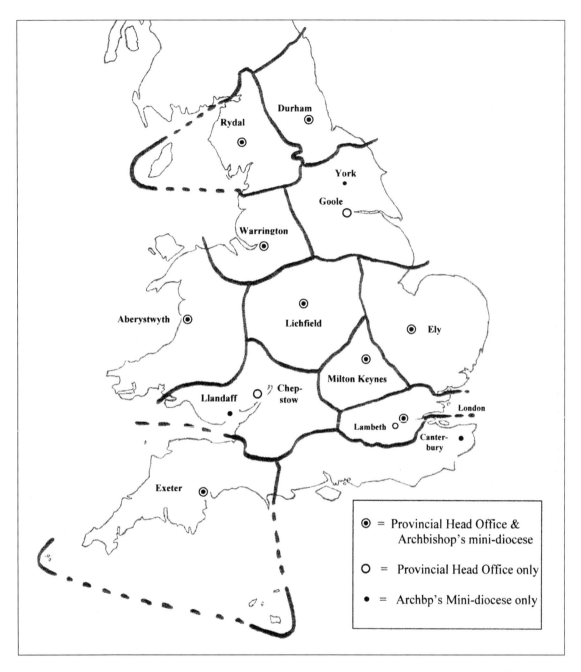

Diagram 12 PROPOSED TWELVE PROVINCES

B – Mission to people in their homes

The modern British "home base"

So what does the home base of the average British family consist of? We saw above that at the height of the Middle Ages it most certainly consisted of a village or rural small town. Many ordinary agricultural workers were bound by force of law to continue living in the village in which they were born. How different is the scene now. Every family belongs in a very real way to a "high street", a town centre where its home life is serviced on at least a weekly basis. This is the place where people go for their banking, multiple shopping needs etc. Such a town centre could be one of many "high streets" strung out every two or three miles across a vast urban area such as London, Birmingham or Cardiff. It could be the centre of an industrial town of 60,000 population, or an ancient rural market town of 2,000 people.[15] This town centre is likely to have a market, a fire station, a public library and a supermarket, if not a branch of Marks and Spencer. The High Street is an important home environment. Anyone who has lived some years in the area will find it hard not to bump into somebody they know every time they go there. Although this is belonging at quite a significant level, there is another home base level of community where most of an individual's relationships will be a bit more significant, especially over time. This place is the village or urban locality. Localities are indicated most often by the existence of a convenience store/newsagent at their centre, plus some postal facilities.

The church structured so as to be in the midst of people's home life

Because the home life of a family remains where the most sense of belonging occurs, the first priority of the church should be properly structured mission to people in their domestic setting. One place where the Church of England is comprehensively not doing this at the moment is in the deep countryside. Congregations in remote villages, who have been used to their own resident vicar for the last 1000 years, are experiencing pastoral frustration. They have to make do with as little as one-sixth of the time of a priest while still continuing to use much the same mode of mission.[16] Such ministers are rushed off their feet; they cannot do more than scratch the surface in any part of their rambling pastoral areas. Little wonder that, from a clergy point of view, such jobs are often the most stress-inducing of any ministry. Rather similar situations can also be found in urban areas: several formerly independent parishes are run as a single pastoral unit with all their church buildings trying to operate as before.

We need to re-organise the church's mission to people in their homes. The Anglican parish (or its equivalent in Free Church and Roman Catholic traditions) needs replacing by a structure that caters for the complicated environment in which a modern British family operates.

Virtually everybody in Britain thinks nothing of travelling to their own particular high street. This can even be the case if, as in mountain areas, it is above ten miles away. In this situation there ought not to be a problem for a truly committed Christian to do such a journey for Christ at least once a week. There are a few rural areas of the country which are genuinely isolated by sea, mountains etc. Otherwise, in the vast majority of cases, the right place for the successor to the basilica of old and the current parish church is alongside the high streets of modern Britain. A new name for this building is called for: "church centre" is what best describes it. Such a church centre would be much better equipped and laid-out than what we are used to finding in most traditional parish churches. There would be good access for car drivers and the disabled; and there would be a flexible space of considerable size for worship and another of similar size for meeting and taking refreshment together. There would be a good sound system, large power-point projector screen with additional monitors wherever required on the premises, a moveable stage, and facilities for worship in both traditional liturgical and modern forms. There would be a reception area, Christian book and audio-visuals shop, chapel for smaller groups, office, counselling and meeting rooms and special crèche and other facilities for young children, kitchen and servery, full disabled and other toilet facilities. The furniture, furnishings and plumbing would be adequate for the fullest celebration of the Christian sacraments including baptism by immersion.

Working in support of church centres would be an average of 15 subsidiary premises acting as chapels/contact points. These would be sited in each locality or village, whose residents, in ordinary life terms, shopped in the town centre. Where a large number of country villages depend on a relatively isolated large town, there could be more than 25 of these subsidiary structures; but where the area was extremely isolated and therefore centred on its principal village, there could be under ten. These structures would be smaller than the parish church as we have known it. Yet in many cases they would be better equipped and more strategically sited than a large number of existing parish churches. Using the analogy of power distribution, "substation" would be a more helpful name for these small local chapel/contact points. The substation would be about 6 metres square with kitchenette and toilet facilities on a scale similar to a simple shop unit. These substations might find they lent themselves to serving as Christian cafes in order to both fill the social gap left by the fall in the number of sub-post offices and to make the gospel more widely available. Where necessary, vandal protection could be built in, as with shops. See Chapter 6 for suggestions as to how substations might be incorporated into existing parish churches in some villages.

Fresh names for fresh forms of mission – "new skins for new wine" Luke 5:38 (RSV)

In order to communicate to the Anglican community that real change was happening, the word "parish" should be scrapped. New names for new forms of mission help to teach people about the nature of the task ahead. Denominations could find it easier to join in outreach (as far as their doctrine allows) if the entire Christian body was going to embark on a venture which was new for all those participating. In some parts of the country existing Roman Catholic parishes could find that they are already about the size of an area proposed to be served by a church centre.

As explained above, the area attached to a church centre would contain up to 25 localities or villages. Such an area would be comparable to the catchment of a comprehensive secondary school in which there are a number of feeder primary schools. Or one could compare it to the land area within certain watersheds which drains into a particular river. As I have borrowed the word substation from the structure used in electricity distribution, so I believe "catchment" is an appropriate name for the area served by a church centre. "Substation" should be a reminder of the power Jesus said his disciples would receive for distribution into every corner of a needy world (see Acts 1:8). "Catchment", though a word for a pastoral area, should unmistakeably remind us of our calling to be fishers of men in large numbers (see John 21:6). A church catchment of today would be nearer in scale to the bishopric of the Roman period than the parish as we have known it. See the map on the next page for an example.

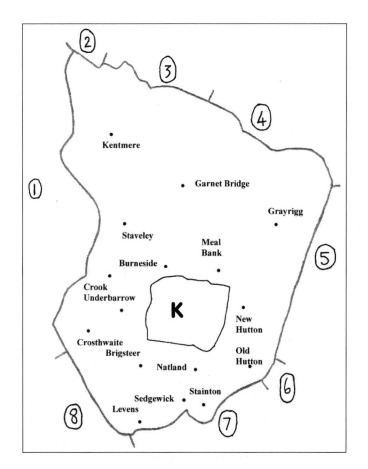

K = Kendal with 7 or
8 substations

. = a substation

CATCHMENTS

1 = Windermere
2 = Penrith
3 = Appleby
4 = Kirkby Stephen
5 = Sedbergh
6 = Kirkby
    Lonsdale
7 = Milnthorpe
8 = Grange-over-
    Sands

Diagram 13   CATCHMENT PROPOSED FOR THE KENDAL AREA

The position of the catchment boundary is influenced not only by the distance of an outlying community from Kendal but also by the "pulling power" of neighbouring towns which would form the centres of adjacent catchments.

Applying the catchment treatment according to how urban areas develop

As cities and towns grow from their original market town status into major industrial and commercial centres, their high streets become less intimate. They become harder to park in and so less convenient for the weekly shopping trip, especially for anyone living further away from the big shops than a short bus ride. At this point secondary high streets are likely to have appeared on several of the main roads into the city or town. These will then be right places for church centres serving catchments of 20-25,000 people. The original town centre may remain the high street for one segment of the city. This would be the obvious site for that segment to have its church centre.

The proposed new structure contrasted with the old "mission to homes" structure

As the Church of England amalgamates more and more ancient parishes into single benefices (pastoral unit under a priest-in-charge), all that has tended to happen is competition between congregations which are too close to each other. Highly mobile churchgoers may simply pick the church in the area that suits them. In many cases they do this without very much regard for the mission of the church to the area in which they live. What we need is missionary purpose and direction that is made clear simply by the way we order our church life. The church centre is proposed as the place for the big weekly celebrations of worship and witness. The substation, by contrast, is the place of contact with people in their homes and immediate locality. It is where committed Christians should gather for a short act of worship before working out lifts for everybody to get to the church centre for the main Sunday Eucharist or other celebration. This Sunday "liturgical bus stop" function is the principal way the substation would support the church centre. Contrast the present situation where there can often be competition between a town centre parish church and a village or suburban parish church. See below in Chapter 4 for a description of how the whole catchment could support the work of the substation with regular "power distribution" in a rich variety of missionary gifts.

Residential mission and church growth

The above is only a brief sketch of how mission to people in their residential community life would be structured. It is perhaps just sufficient to begin to build a picture of the church repositioned alongside the complex web of life that goes to make up the modern region. The business of evangelisation should not stop when a new convert to the Christian way is made. Growth in numbers becomes fruitless without growth in outward-looking discipleship. The success of the church in the first three centuries (and 18th century Methodism and 21st century Pentecostalism) is all about one-to-one discipling and work in small cell groups that is strongly built into church life. The church would grow better if it contained fewer partial and stunted converts. The above proposals for replacing the parish are designed to lighten the burden of inherited structure, especially of buildings. With less historic baggage, clergy and congregations could be freer to improve their discipling. With less heritage to administer, there would be more time to use well-tried biblical methods of Christian growth (ie both in personal Christ-likeness and in numbers).

C – Mission to people when away from their home base

Regions and provinces

At present the Church of England divides into two provinces: Canterbury in the south and York in the north. This once had a lot to do with the fact that in the sixth century the mission to regain this country for Christ came from Scotland and the Continent at almost the same time. But one cannot help feeling that continuing with the two-province arrangement does not have a lot to do with our current missionary task. Are not Anglicans in fact clinging to the present arrangement because it makes a statement that theirs is the "ancient and original" church of the land? Though I am myself an Anglican, I have to confess that we would look a lot more "catholic and apostolic" if our provincial layout showed that we were properly geared up for doing our catholic and apostolic missionary work. We should be doing it as if we meant business within God's creation as it actually exists in the UK today! We have some things to learn here from the provincial structure that arose when three churches united in the 1970s and 1980s to form the United Reformed

Church. The regional structures of the Baptists and Assemblies of God also have a savour of present-day relevance about them.

At such a time as this when our society gets deafer by the year to the Word of God, provinces should be put to work in the world of today. Regions are very complex: in a real sense they contain the "whole framework of the human order" (compare Mark 16:15 in section A above). Regions cry out for church "provinces" to enable the Christian body to be fully and efficiently present in and alongside that whole framework. A province, of the same general dimensions as a region, should consist of up to a dozen dioceses. The archbishop and his team of diocesan bishops would hold together the aspects of the church's mission within the province. In particular they would see that mission to people in their work life was properly linked to mission to them in their home life. The arrangements for this would be as described in the next section.[17]

The church's mission to people in their work life

a) Ministry to profit-making and public service industries and higher education found within the province would be led for the whole province by one of the diocesan bishops, assisted by one or two of his fellow bishops. Such ministry, which has been known for some time as "sector ministry", would often fall within the confines of one province. Where it didn't, the team in charge would need to include one or more representatives from the leadership of the relevant neighbouring province(s).

b) Local government services such as refuse collection are performed by an authority which covers an area bigger than a catchment but usually smaller than a county. A diocese should roughly correspond to this intermediate grouping of residential towns. Each diocese would be under the sole leadership of its bishop for purposes of residential mission. Dioceses would be less bulky in administrative terms than existing Church of England dioceses. They would share office and specialist facilities within a province. Provincial synod would replace the present diocesan synods, but each bishop would have his own council and budget for residential mission. There would be no need of suffragan bishops. A diocese would contain up to 25 catchments. It would in many cases occupy a segment of the province converging on a centrally positioned archdiocese. The diocese could be the unit into which the monastic life was integrated. This would help bring the gift and witness of monks and nuns into close contact with residential mission, especially if there were sufficient members of active religious orders to have a leadership/specialist role in a fair proportion of the catchments at any given time. Diocesan boundaries would be alterable by provincial synod. Bishops could site their cathedra (principal chair of office) where they chose within their dioceses.

c) There would be a small archdiocese that ideally would occupy the centre of the province. It would contain no more than five catchments. The archbishop could thus keep in close touch with some residential church life. With the other archbishops he would share in speaking the Word of God to the nation as a whole. The team of archbishops would be responsible for liaising with other Christian bodies across Europe to provide united ministry to international commuters (see Chapter 8 for more on this new phenomenon now commonplace since the growth of air travel). An archbishop would also co-operate in seeing that aspects of mission that straddled two or more provinces were carried out smoothly. Examples of this might be witness and ministry to users of motorway service areas, relations with the national media, and involvement in Parliament and other national institutions. Where statute law is failing to empower society to act against criminal behaviour or other injustice, the churches need to have a voice and an arm to campaign for it to be changed. Teamwork by or on behalf of 12 archbishops would go a long way towards dealing with this area of witness and work for the Kingdom of God. Often national self-help groups spring up to combat injustice, and the church should be there alongside to listen and support whatever is true and righteous. There needs to be a strong ecumenical team to uphold Bible truth for the nation(s), and to challenge those responsible when this is not presented properly in the media.[18]

d) Existing cathedrals, large abbey churches and retreat houses would be administered as a resource for the whole province.

The relationship between sector and parish ministries has not always been positive in the Anglican churches in the UK. Because rightly structured provinces could provide an overview, they should be used as a channel of communication between residential and sector ministry. Provinces would be in the business of maintaining up-to-date records of where lay Christians are working. They would need to discern whether there were any key members of the Body of Christ who needed releasing from commitments in catchments so as to be more available as leaders of Christian work and witness in their workplace. Just as parish clergy are currently called upon to defer to chaplaincy work going on within their parishes, so clergy and some congregation members from each catchment would need to co-operate in supporting the sector mission of the province. They would need to be drawn into provincial prayer meetings to help discern the Lord's calling of certain members of their congregations to reshape their time-commitments in favour of sector mission.[19]

D – The re-use of old church premises of any denomination for any structure needed in province or catchment

In various traditions, including the Anglican one, a building that is to be used as a place of worship has been consecrated or dedicated for the giving of glory exclusively to God the Holy Trinity. In a significant number of Anglican church buildings this consecration has over the centuries been compromised. A common example of this is the inclusion of stones that carry pagan inscriptions in the fabric of church buildings. Such practices, which grieve the Holy Spirit, have had the effect of keeping him from coming upon the congregation to help them to grow spiritually and spread the gospel. The Old Testament is full of instances where the Israelite people became poor and oppressed because they gave space in their lives to idols as well as to the true God. Alien anti-gospel forces must not be allowed to have their own investment in our worship buildings. See Nehemiah 2:10, 6:1-14, and 13:1-9, where Tobiah the Ammonite, an enemy of the People of God, had wormed his way into the Temple Precincts and had got himself granted a room there. His furniture was thrown out and that section of the holy place was duly cleansed and restored to its proper use.

Therefore before any redevelopment of old church premises takes place, a full praying through, testing, and spiritual mapping of the site needs to be carried out by all denominations who are investing in the project. Just as a purchaser of a house needs to have a survey done for defects, so other denominations need to do a spiritual survey before acquiring a stake in a shared building. Investment must not be wasted and people who are seeking to set forward the work of the gospel must not be needlessly discouraged. All idolatrous practices, connections and works that are discovered need to be repented of, renounced and removed, with the ministry of deliverance, cleansing and re-consecrating carried out jointly. The name of the one and only Saviour, the Lord Jesus Christ, should then be lifted up by all concerned in the project.

There are deep feelings embedded in the nation when it comes to the subject of redeveloping ancient buildings. Therefore following Chapters 3 and 4, which will look further at the proposed provinces and catchments, Chapter 5 will confront the great issue of heritage in relation to the gospel.

E – Chart to show how the proposed changes would look for Anglicans

		CURRENT STRUCTURES	PROPOSED STRUCTURES
Geographical area	Smaller / Larger	Several **parishes/benefices**	Many **substations** One **catchment**
		One **deanery**	About three **catchments**
		One **diocese** (currently overseeing much of existing sector, ie non-residential ministry)	Several lightweight **dioceses** each with oversight of residential mission
		Three **provinces**	Many lightweight **dioceses** Twelve **provinces** each having primary oversight over non-residential mission

CHAPTER 3   THE 12 PROPOSED PROVINCES SEEN IN CONTEXT

The present national structures of the churches in southern UK differ one from another as shown in the samples illustrated in diagrams 19 and 20 later in this chapter. Current Anglican structure for southern UK relates strongly to the traditional county boundaries as in the map below.[20]

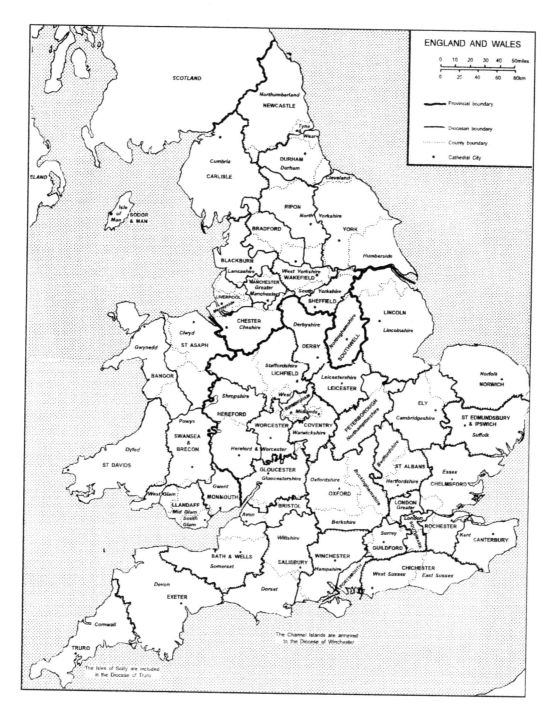

Diagram 14   ANGLICAN ENGLAND & WALES: THE CURRENT SHAPE[21]

These current Anglican boundaries coincide with the Scottish border but not quite with the Welsh. They do have immediate relevance to some local government areas. They do not however cater for the whole life zone as explained above.

In outlining life zones we are not going to be able simply to borrow some actual current boundaries in the manner of Anglican dioceses using county areas. Different national bodies wanting to work with regions carve up the country in somewhat different ways. Yet there is a generally recognised way of doing it, and variations are usually due to what is marginally more economic and convenient for the task in hand. For example, northern Cumbria is likely to gravitate towards Tyneside for some services rather than towards Manchester, because it is area of relatively small population isolated by its mountains. Southern Cumbria is isolated by the terrain from northern Cumbria and feels much more part of the North-West than the North-East.

In looking to fit church provinces to regions, there would have to be some attention paid to what can be fitted together as a domestic church unit which is not too unwieldy. Other agencies do this, without of course losing sight of the fact that business has to be about identifying with the needs of consumers. Church structures from of old can, in some instances, be incorporated in modern ones. This is a good policy so long as it does not stop us doing the real job of coming alongside today's communities. Part, but only part, of the witness of the church is the fact that we have some history behind us.

As explained in Chapter 2, there are a number of indicators of regions including motorways and television. With all these points in mind, the following twelve provinces would appear relevant to the task the church now faces:

NAME OF PROVINCE	TYPE	MAJOR ESTUARY(S)	ARCHBISHOP'S TITLE	HEAD OFFICE
London	Radial	Yes	London	The City
Mid-South	Radial		Milton Keynes	Milton Keynes
Mid-West	Bifocal	Yes	Llandaff	Chepstow
North-West	Bifocal	Yes	Warrington	Warringon
North-East	Bifocal	Yes	Durham	Durham
Humbria	Bifocal	Yes	York	Goole
Midlands	Trifocal		Lichfield	Lichfield
South	Linear (Continental links)	Yes	Canterbury	Lambeth

NAME OF PROVINCE	TYPE	MAJOR ESTUARY(S)	ARCHBISHOP'S TITLE	HEAD OFFICE
Lakes, Dales & Man	Lungs of the nation		Rydal	Rydal
Cambria	Lungs of the nation		Aberystwyth	Aberystwyth
South-West	Lungs of the nation		Exeter	Exeter
East Anglia	Agricultural		Ely	Ely

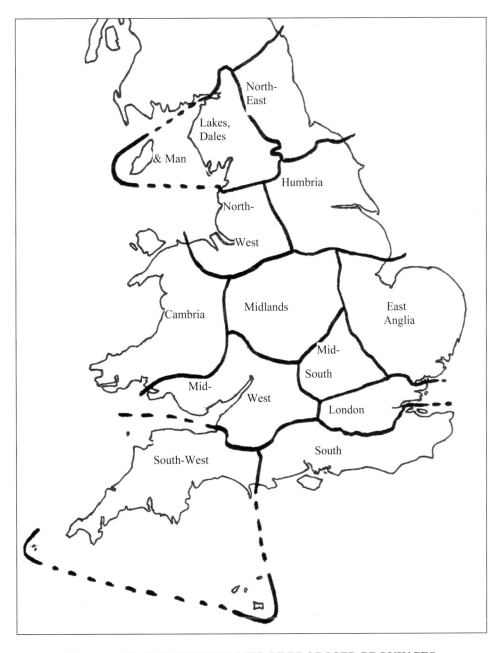

Diagram 15   MAP WITH NAMES OF PROPOSED PROVINCES

Comparison of the 12 proposed provinces with 3 structures found in the nation's life

By way of a check on the appropriateness of the above, comparisons with three present-day regional structures are provided in the diagrams below.

Road transport

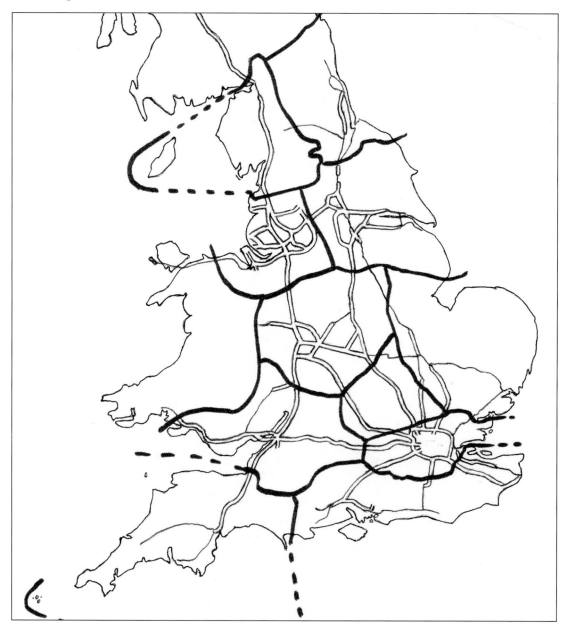

 Boundaries of proposed provinces (also on next 2 pages)
Motorways
Dual carriageways linking or extending the national motorway network (NB portions of A66 still not made dual)

Diagram 16   MAP OF PROVINCES COMPARED WITH MOTORWAY NETWORK

46

Regional television

ITV regions compare closely with the proposed provinces. In particular, over the years some have operated either side of the Scottish and Welsh borders. BBC TV Regions are compared in the map below:

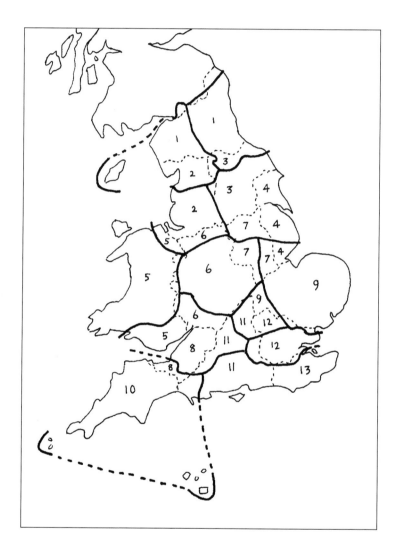

BBC TV REGIONS

1	North East & Cumbria
2	North West
3	Yorkshire
4	East Yorks & Lincs
5	Wales
6	West Midlands
7	East Midlands
8	West
9	East
10	South West
11	South
12	London
13	South East

- - - approx TV regions

Diagram 17 MAP OF PROPOSED PROVINCES COMPARED WITH BBC TV REGIONS[22]

Government regions

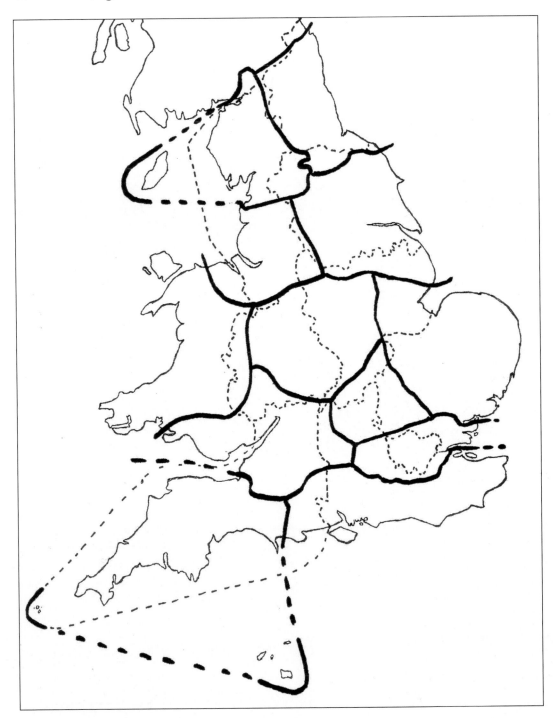

- - - - Boundaries of government regions

Diagram 18   MAP OF PROVINCES COMPARED WITH GOVERNMENT REGIONS[23]

48

A similar comparison with six current church structures

On the next two pages are maps that compare the current structure used by six different denominations with the proposed provinces.

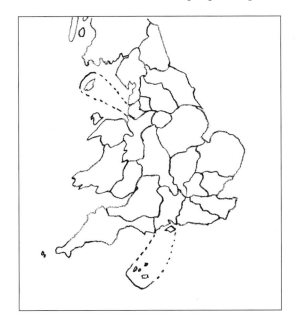

Roman Catholic dioceses[24]

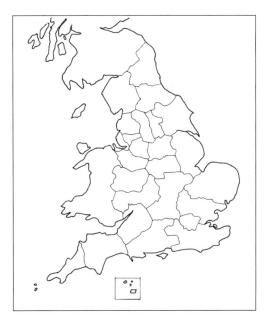

Methodist districts[25]

Baptist regions[26]

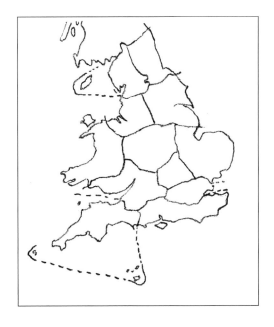

Proposed provinces

**Diagram 19   PRESENT STRUCTURES OF RC, METHODIST & BAPTIST REGIONS
COMPARED WITH A MAP OF THE PROPOSED PROVINCES**

United Reformed regions[27]

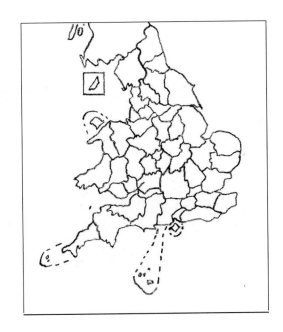

Anglican dioceses[28]

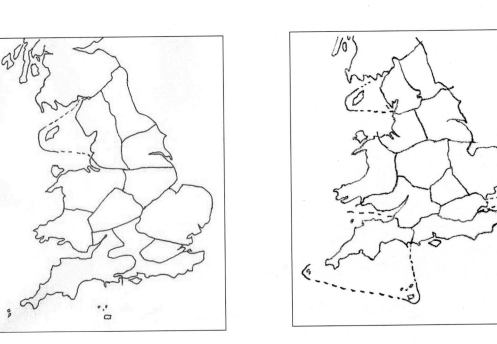

Assemblies of God regions[29]

Proposed provinces

**Diagram 20   PRESENT STRUCTURES OF URC, ANGLICAN & AOG REGIONS
COMPARED WITH A MAP OF THE PROPOSED PROVINCES**

Commentary on the 12 proposed provinces

London, Mid-South & Midlands

Mid-South admittedly includes towns well within normal commuting range of London. It has been proposed as a way of relieving the pressure of trying to have the whole of the Thames basin in one province. It also allows Midlands Province to be less bulky. Redundant church buildings in London might be found that were suitable for redevelopment as the Head Office of London Province. This could either help save some worthwhile architecture or make better use of a site which no longer served a residential area well.[30]

Mid-West

The fact that this province is in both England and Wales affirms the economic and social reality of a region which has the Bristol Channel/Severn Estuary as its hub. Chepstow is central for administrative purposes. Llandaff has a particular place in the history of British Christianity. As a diocese it can be continuously traced back, via a name change in 1121, to AD 560.[31] It therefore makes a suitable area for an archbishop's mini-diocese.

North-West

Perhaps the full name of this province ought to be North-West Anew as it has "Also North East Wales" in it. Manweb was invented for a similar function in the electricity industry. For the same reason as Mid-West, North-West straddles a national boundary. (We may note that national boundaries are already transgressed by many organisations including the Baptist and Anglican churches, and The Assemblies of God.) Because Manchester and Merseyside are the two largest conurbations of the region, it makes sense, as in other bifocal provinces to locate the centre of authority at a central point, in this case Warrington. This town is also central to the motorway network.

North-East

Again, economic and social reality dictates that the northern border of the province does not have to stick slavishly to national borders. The border of the 44 dioceses of the Church of England already fails to respect national boundaries in a number of places.

Humbria & South

For the sake of continuity with early church history, York and Canterbury could be retained as names/dioceses of the archbishops of these two provinces. However provincial headquarters would need to be in more focused locations, both for convenience of travel and for the sense of belonging felt by the whole province. As it happens, Lambeth is extremely central to South province if one is using rail links.

South

South Province is linear in the sense that it does not have a natural centre within itself. The M27 is perhaps an attempt to create a linear unity for the region on which this province is based. The separate existence of South Province has the benefit of allowing London

Province to be kept to a reasonable size. It also allows the Southampton conurbation to be recognised as separate from London. One important common industry throughout South Province is transport to the Continent; another is seaside and international tourism especially of the day-trip variety. Having Canterbury as the mini-diocese city is historically appropriate and does no organisational harm if Lambeth is developed as head office.

Midlands

The Birmingham, Potteries and Nottingham/Leicester areas are the main conurbations of this region; and they need a central focus. Lichfield is geographically in this central position. It also has a long history as a bishop's headquarters. As such, it is an appropriate place for the head office of Midlands Province.

Lakes, Dales & Man

Neither of the two mainland parts of this region could fit happily with an adjacent large conurbation. Their economic interests are so different from those of heavily built-up areas. Along with the Isle of Man they also share geographical isolation from such big centres. The major industry here is tourism. This is clearly centred on sea, mountain, moorland & lake scenery. Great care is rightly taken by the National Parks within this region to conserve the resources on which this industry depends, including fresh air, clean rivers and plenty of peace and quiet. A small section of Scotland is more isolated from Scottish towns than from the border city of Carlisle. It is therefore included in this province.

Cambria

This province has similarities to Lakes, Dales & Man. It excludes those parts in the north of Wales which are socially and economically linked to Northwest Province. Likewise it excludes those parts of South Wales which are Bristol Channel oriented. However it includes a section of the English Marches which are a tourist area remote from the large conurbations of the English Midlands. Cambria, with a centrally placed headquarters at Aberystwyth, includes most of the territory in which Welsh is used as a first language.

South-West

This holiday and retirement area includes the Channel Islands and again has similarities to both of the above two provinces.

East Anglia

This is the only life zone where farming and all that goes with it is the biggest industry. There are various cities of moderate size throughout this region. Ely, though small, fulfils the need for a central headquarters. As in the case of Lichfield it also has a fairly long history as a city with a bishop attached.

CHAPTER 4   THE CATCHMENT EXPLORED IN MORE DETAIL

Church centres and substations

As explained above, the residential mission of the church should be centred where people's home life is serviced. Although food shopping, and some leisure shopping, is now often done at out-of-town supermarkets, the high street is still an important focus. In particular, it is where most specialist products and services are found together within walking distance. The town high street is therefore where church centres should normally be placed. At present in the Church of England this is so often not the case in regard to parish churches; these tend to be in (but sometimes outside!) nearly every ancient village, near a town's castle, left behind as the town centre has developed and moved, or lost in the middle of a large housing development without reference to other community structures. This last feature dates from the period of urban growth in the early 19th century when the assumption seems to have been made that large towns were but a series of villages all close together and all requiring the construction of a parish church, simply by virtue of the number of dwellings occupying a particular patch of ground. This approach survived intact until the 1960s.

In cases where an existing parish church or other similar Christian place of worship already exists on or very near a high street, facilities would generally need upgrading to enable the church to operate as a church centre.

In urban areas and villages, the substation should be adjacent to where the people of the locality are serviced. This is likely to be close to a sub-post office in much of the urban scene and in larger villages. In some urban areas and in smaller villages substations should be wherever the natural focus is. This, for example, might be adjacent to the school, pub, telephone kiosk, newsagent or bus stop. It needs to be convenient as a collection point for the giving of lifts, and ideally it should be able to witness easily to the community. This will be the case if it is adjacent to where that community goes about everyday life: withdrawing its cash, collecting its newspapers, transporting children from school etc. Significant numbers of parish churches currently do not fulfil this witnessing role because they are too distant from the place where the community gathers for its everyday functions. Such buildings still cost a lot of money and effort to maintain. What our society needs is inexpensive yet more plentiful subsidiary chapels that act as shop windows/meeting points. These should be highly accessible to everyone in the local residential community, whether they be aged 6 or 86, car owners, or friends who have come by train to stay for the weekend. In an urban area a typical substation might be a rented shop in the same arcade as the sub-post office.

Catchment clergy

In Chapter 2 it was noted how what were formerly independent parishes have been grouped together to form single pastoral units. Some of these have been staffed by teams of clergy. The result has often been an over-emphasis on maintenance of unfilled buildings and lack of pastoral continuity between one full-time minister and a congregation – a recipe for decline. By contrast, the catchment would be so constructed that it used a clergy team but at the same time kept pastoral care continuous. It would link clergy of incumbent status (ie fully trained leadership) in rather the same way as a firm of accountants or solicitors links its partners. The church centre would be where all the clergy and committed worshippers gather at least weekly. As with partners in a firm who have their own clients, each incumbent would have a defined geographical pastorate and be in overall charge of evangelistic and pastoral work of the localities within that pastorate.

Operation and use of substations

As mentioned in Chapter 2, the substation in each locality would operate as a liturgical bus stop for the committed worshippers of the locality or village. These would gather at the substation on a Sunday morning and on the occasion of other major church centre celebrations. An hour before the service in the church centre, the substation bell would be rung for morning or evening praise. While this informal office was in progress, perhaps with accompanying musical instruments, those with and without cars would congregate in and around the substation. About half an hour before the church centre service, committed worshippers would proceed by car to the town centre. The unattached young children who wished to stay for a short Christian instruction would be catered for by a group of local church members. Members of this group would be released from this task by turns so as to be able to attend the start of the church centre service on some occasions. Unattached minors would need parental consent to travel on the same basis as for any modern-day youth outing. Uncommitted enquirers who wished to attend quarter of an hour's morning praise would of course be welcome.

The substation is a somewhat new proposal and as such would need to develop its own appropriate leadership ministry. It would be wise to draw on the experience of a variety of traditions of unpaid local ministry in this country and in the developing world. (In many countries not even six village congregations can support their own full time ordained minister). Substation leaders would need to be trained in pastoral care and supervision of simple worship. To fulfil such a role a person with a more permanent status than an Anglican churchwarden would be needed. This is because churchwardens can be voted out after one year. On the other hand, a permanently appointed cleric would carry the possibility of empire building without regard to the total mission of the catchment. Rotating offices of warden and assistant warden of the substation, which had to change personnel every four years, could be about right. Church members in no more than deacon's orders could be eligible.

Several times a year each locality or village in the catchment would be the venue of a major outreach rally. These rallies would probably be held in the evenings except at weekends in high summer when they could be open-airs in the afternoon. Evening rallies would not necessarily take place in the substation, though the preparatory prayer for them probably would. One would hope this venue would be too small for the actual outreach event! Advance publicity would be provided by the committed worshippers of the locality. Christian teams drawn from across the whole catchment would lead worship, testimony, preaching, healing ministry and counselling. Evangelistic rallies in the substation localities would include the opportunity for confession of faith[32] with all the necessary back-up of mature lay Christians to befriend and counsel new converts. Much current preaching in traditional liturgical services lacks this ingredient.

Substations would be appropriate places for incumbent members of the catchment partnership to say Daily Offices on a rota basis, though no doubt some of this ministerial discipline would take place at the church centre. It would depend on the terms of the partnership agreement between the incumbents.

Catchment structure

As with partnerships of solicitors etc, the senior partner would exercise a presiding and leadership role. The existence of the church centre premises and any specialist staff would operate like cement across the catchment. Shared specialist resources can do this in any organisation. By contrast, under many present multi-church team arrangements there can be tensions when one team vicar wants to be more independent and effectively tries to turn one church with its pastoral area back to single parish status. Specialist staff in a catchment could include youth and community workers, and also people to run the finance and administration who could be in permanent deacon's orders. There would be opportunities for training assistant clergy who could be attached pastorally to any of the partners in the team. Catchments, at about a third of the size and more muscular than Anglican deaneries, would render the latter obsolete.

A catchment synod would replace present Anglican PCCs and deanery synods. Each locality would be furnished with whatever small committee it needed, appointed partly locally, partly by catchment synod, and partly on an ex officio basis.

Rural pastorates

In the early stages of developing the catchment structure in the countryside, full-time clergy would best be housed within their pastorates, outside the town but a convenient distance from it, but not right in any of the villages, which had previously contained a parish church. This would help in the breaking down of the village expectation that a parson should be their exclusive possession.[33]

The reasons behind the proposal that the catchment replace previous structures

These are shown along with relevant notes in a table on the next page. They have a honourable pedigree in another setting – the life's work of Field Marshall Viscount Montgomery of Alamein. He experienced outmoded strategy being used in the First World War and set about preparing up-to date-strategy for use in the Second World War.[34]

We need the catchment because:

It allows for a **flexible response** to the current missionary task.	The complex and evolving shape of residential life requires **flexibility**. We need a **large enough missionary unit** (a) to achieve a critical mass of servant believers in every district, (b) to move resources easily to where they are needed for regular periodic mission and (c) to relate to and co-operate with sector ministries, such as industrial mission, both on a local and a provincial scale. Currently the Church of England tries to respond to the missionary task by continuing to use the **rigid** parish system. However it is being forced to keep planning for further **retreat** because of lack of resources to pay clergy.
It is **economical** in numbers of congregations of celebration size that need to be maintained.	Laity need to belong to a church which leaves them **time** to spend with their families and with non-believers. The time they do give needs spending more on mission, less on maintenance. Keen laity already travel to all manner of Christian meetings and conferences. The catchment system invites them to do it as a normal part of their discipleship in a way that is in line with their existing everyday life. **Waste** of spiritual life and exhaustion in trying to maintain a failing system is even more serious for the clergy. In too many posts they are expected to man a long line of static buildings and structures where there is little hope of breakthrough. The catchment is about energy saving **co-operation** over a wide area.
It provides bigger and better equipped church centres that can be **attractive** to a population mobile enough to shop around.	Such church centres could offer people the chance to celebrate God's greatness. TV Songs of Praise provides such a celebration electronically on Sunday evenings. Why can't the church do it in the flesh throughout the country every Sunday morning? Glory in worship **attracts**. Church centres could provide better **pulling power** for teenagers, who expect to find their entertainment in the town centre, are culturally attuned to larger gatherings, and are always wanting the chance to meet up with their friends.
As a framework for effective mission it allows for better **value for money** spent on the upkeep of buildings.	**Substations** are inherently much smaller and cheaper than parish churches. They could therefore be placed more comprehensively in the centre of all the nation's localities. This is something the parish church was supposed to have achieved, but since the time of William the Conqueror probably never has. (He was very keen on a comprehensive system; every little place with 100 or more population had to have its own vicar! And of course His Majesty was the patron for all the new mini-parish appointments this policy required.... = a very neat spy network against the king's enemies). Substations are designed to be front-line outposts. In post-Christian society parish churches too easily become "clubhouses half a mile from the action". Rightly led, the substation would have a praying body of believers to be the heart and hands, ears and vocal chords of Christ locally. We need local **intelligence**, not for King William the Conqueror, but for the work of God's kingdom. Intelligence for the Kingdom of God includes discovering who has what need in a locality, but also requires discernment of, and dealing with, the **unseen** enemies of the gospel.[35]

The notes attached to the above four reasons for proposing the catchment system leave no room for doubt: we need lay discipline. Christian mission led by John Wesley required it in the 18th century: the early Methodist class system enabled the church to operate at more than one organised level. A motivated laity disciplined for mission is what our western society needs if it is to be reclaimed for Christ. A two-level missionary life for the church has been likened to a bird that has at last recovered its lost wing and so is able to fly again.[36]

Montgomery believed that fighting was everyone's task. Europe's church is based far too much on the cruise liner principle. Every member ministry, or body ministry, where the spiritual work is not mainly left to the clergy but is a shared enterprise, is needed on a widespread scale if our continent is to be re-Christianised. Cell church principles are an essential part of this renewal of spiritual life; in this way of thinking the church is a hospital where those who come in on crutches and carrying old junk go out fit and free to work in the Kingdom. The church that is carrying old junk provides in its corporate life a very bad model for the individual who needs to become free of it in Christ. Europe could learn from the church in China which, where it was dispossessed by the Communists, went underground and grew wonderfully.

A generation ago Anglican Confirmation operated to a large extent as a gateway to communion. For the vast majority this was little more than a reverent custom at puberty, similar to the reverent national tradition of baptism in infancy. It has already lost much of this role and become more rare in the process. Confirmation has become more closely linked to commitment to Christ within the church, whenever the Spirit brings that about in an individual's life. For it to move away from being so much of a rite of passage, and a little closer to its scriptural origins, is a positive development. Yet it would still be good to see Confirmation relieved altogether of its place as a gateway to communion. In addition it could usefully be unshackled from trying to serve as the means of entering the fullness of the life of the Spirit. For this it is rather too formal and rigid. Would it not therefore be better to see Confirmation recycled as an adult commitment to mission? It could be the point when an individual accepts missionary discipline and receives the bishop's laying on of hands for work within the total outreach of the church. If, to begin with, we had to work with small numbers of disciplined Christians, would that be such a hardship? In many congregations the proportion of members committed to mission is not so very great now.

How may we sum up the reasons for proposing a catchment system to replace the parish system?

We need to use a missionary approach which is very local and can give back to the homes of our nation a close pastoral care comparable to that once enjoyed by the whole population at the hands of a plentiful professional clergy. We also need church centres which do a comprehensive, quality job for a town and its area. In the gospel sphere we should be providing a service comparable to that provided in the shopping sphere by a town's High Street. People can buy a rich variety of quality food and clothing. The Bible has things to say about pastoring and feeding the sheep, and "putting on Christ". The church should gear itself up to meet these spiritual needs in the population. The catchment could have a greater capacity to do this than our worn-out parish. The catchment system is more local than the parish often is. Yet it is also designed to concentrate, and make better use of, scarce church resources in a post-Christian society.

CHAPTER 5   THE GOSPEL AND HERITAGE

"Since we are surrounded... let us throw off everything that hinders" Hebrews 12:1 (NIV)

The breadth of our Christian heritage and the nation's affection for it

As in other parts of Europe, there is in Britain an inheritance of church structures belonging to various denominations. These church structures consist of geographical provinces, dioceses, circuits etc as well as church buildings. In the mind of the nation as a whole, it is the heritage of church buildings that matters most, with the possible exception of the role of archbishops. In and around cathedral cities there is, granted, some feeling in the local community for the existence of a bishop having been based at the cathedral over centuries. However any idea of what a diocese, district or province consists of passes by the average man in the street.

Geographical areas of Christian work and those in charge of them (Christian work structures)

Britain has a Christian history going back to the period of the Roman Empire. There were at least two bishops in Britain in the fourth century, some 90 years before the end of Roman rule. The heathen invasions of the early Dark Ages all but wiped out the church structure that had begun to form in the Roman period. Thus the oldest church structures in present-day use effectively date from the re-Christianisation of Britain in the sixth century AD. For southern Britain these are the areas of work known as the Anglican provinces of Wales, York and Canterbury.

There are probably relatively few Christians who care deeply about the continuation of the existing boundaries at diocesan or district level. Many worshipping Christians would not grieve for long over the altering of church boundaries of county size. Some would feel it if provinces were created that straddled national boundaries significantly. Such a course could be seen as a threat to national identity. Generally though, the main barrier to changing boundaries is inertia. The upheaval, cost, and legal adjustments needed to effect change through Parliament are all to be measured against the gain of a streamlined church refocused for mission in priority to maintenance. Because of either changed trading conditions or human failures, businesses can find themselves facing annihilation; unless they are restructured they die. There is no gain without pain. The church is likewise faced with a choice. It should have the edge over business because it professes to believe in the resurrection of Jesus from the dead. This was the greatest ever instance of gain with pain.

Structures consisting of church buildings

If boundaries have a hold on the affections of only a few people, with church buildings it is a different story. Nearly all of us feel attachment to buildings, even though we are less attached to realistic giving towards their upkeep. The rest of this chapter, together with Chapter 6, is largely devoted to seeing how we can conserve our buildings heritage in a realistic, gospel-minded way. The author believes that currently we are not facing up to what is involved in viable conservation for the long term.

In southern Britain the Anglican church has the largest heritage of church buildings, most of which serve an ancient parish system as parish churches. The majority are either original Gothic from the Middle Ages or built in the Gothic style in the 19th century. The Methodist Church is the only other denomination which has a comparable array of church buildings, and many of these are in 19th century Gothic style. The interior furnishing of most of these buildings is still stuck in the 19th century. This was the last time re-ordering and refurbishment of the interior layout took place in most Anglican buildings.

If we study the full breadth of our Christian heritage, we find that a far richer tradition of building use has existed in earlier times. It is interesting to note that in the rather few cases where our church buildings have been re-ordered and given a fresh interior layout, many things have been reintroduced which were considered necessary in previous Christian eras. I refer to examples such as good catering facilities, a variety of room sizes instead of one big room, a raised stage or platform close to the congregation, and room to move about rather than all the space taken up with fixed seating. The places where re-ordering has been done in a way that is adequate to the needs of a lively Christian community have so far been few in number. This has usually been because the resources have not been there unless the ministry of a local church has outstripped its parish boundary or other given area of operation. In other words, it has cornered the market and beaten other local churches to it! Can it be that such churches have just got on with carving out their own version of a catchment system?

The challenge Christians are facing

Because we believe in the Communion of Saints we are to take notice of the witness of Christians in former ages as well as the witness of modern-day Christians in all parts of the world. We need them to help us run the gospel "race that is set before us" (RSV).[37]

The tradition of the first three centuries (no buildings to speak of, but glorious expansion), the growth of hidden, unofficial churches in recent years, and the heritage of expansion outside Western Europe all speak God's call to us to go for growth. Of course our situation differs from most of these other saints in that in our case the heritage buildings are already there. We therefore need a faith that ensures that these buildings are not the god which governs how we do God's mission. When Jesus told us to be careful not to worship money he meant that for some this would mean giving up all their money literally; for most though it means not serving money but serving God with money.[38]

As we need to put money (mammon) in its place, so we need to put precious old buildings in their place according to the values of God's kingdom. A true-to-life example of what happens when we serve the mammon of precious old buildings can be seen in the following (fictional) advert details, typical of the 1990s, when a new priest was needed to take charge of six country churches:

The small town of Wandlesham and four nearby villages are located 11 miles from a cathedral city. Each village has an historic parish church. There is already in place a team of four unpaid leaders (local ministers and readers) holding a bishop's licence. The town, which contains the one big church, has a rural industry which is the major employer. Otherwise most people commute into the city for work and for nearly all shopping. The population of the whole place including the villages is under 2500. There is a church primary school. The advert seeks a new vicar who will fit in with the local desire to keep all the churches going and who will work with all ages.

There is mention of the different individual communities, but no mention of "working together for mission". This is in marked contrast to the French publication, mentioned later in Chapter 7, entitled "Collaborer pour la Mission" (*Working together for mission).* In this document it is frankly admitted that the majority of existing parishes are incapable on their own of (a) nourishing Christians (b) mobilising them in mission.[39]

The Wandlesham case would be very different if the same population were concentrated in one small urban locality. Then, according to modern standards of urban parish staffing, this population might expect to receive under half the time of a paid priest and perhaps a small part of the time of one of the licensed unpaid leaders. So the Wandlesham Group is asking for more gospel resources on the basis, not of more people, but of more buildings heritage.

What does "work with all ages" mean? One can fairly say that it betrays how difficult it is for hardworking members scattered through the six churches to make inroads into most sections of modern society. Young people are probably top of their problem list.

As far as the saints who built our ancient buildings are concerned, we best relate to them today by glorifying Jesus and treating those buildings as Jesus would have us do today. Some of these buildings, and certainly some of the contents of most of them, were put in place for the glory of men rather than of Jesus. For an example of gospel work done for the wrong motives we may refer to Philippians 1:15. The saints who put up our old buildings were sinners as we are. Now that they are purified and glorious in the presence of Jesus, they will rejoice to see alterations to the heritage they left for us which are in line with the values of Jesus.

By gospel standards, some parts of our buildings heritage were indeed flawed at the start. Yet we should still recognise that ancient buildings are a valid part of witness to the Christian faith. Our trouble is that we have allowed them to become the tail that wags the dog. They divert many members of congregations from actively spreading the gospel.

In Jesus' parable of the Wicked Tenants in Luke 20:14b we hear the words, "Let us kill him that the inheritance may be ours." (RSV) To focus on heritage and to deny the owner his rights is a serious sin. There may be no intention to push Christ out. Those however in the church who are believers should have spreading the gospel as their overriding priority.

In Matthew 22:15-22, the Pharisees joined forces with the Jewish puppet political establishment to try and trap Jesus with a trick question on whether or not taxes should be paid to the Roman Empire. Secretly they hated being under Roman rule. They longed for a restoration of Israeli sovereignty after the style of their golden age some nine centuries previously. But God had already said to them in their scriptures that they had no need to restore their golden age. Provided that the pagan empire under which they lived allowed them to worship him, God had already said that they were to concentrate on being his servant to bring his light to the world around them. The answer Jesus gave them, "Give to Caesar what is Caesar's" (ie the Empire's) "and give to God what is God's" (NIV) took them by surprise. The question Jesus was facing them with was, "are you willing to follow the teaching of God in Isaiah 42, 45, 49, 52 and 53 where the new role for God's people is defined?"

We similarly are not called to fight to restore what was built by saints of old, but to work with God to serve the gospel in today's world. A small part of that service is to assist our heritage of ancient buildings to speak a word of faith from the past, without destroying gospel faith in the present. The more sensitively our ancient buildings are integrated into the business of currently sharing the gospel, the more clearly they speak of that gospel. If we let the non-gospel-believing state run them, their witness will be impaired. This has already happened in France where nearly all parish churches belong to the state.[40]

England and Wales contain a wealth of ancient church buildings. The majority of these are Anglican. The burden has remained far more on the shoulders of the congregations using these buildings than is the case by comparison with many other parts of Western Europe. It might be thought that the more government finance that can be put into our heritage of ancient buildings the better. This is not necessarily the case, because with state money for historic churches come state strings (eg the strict conditions required by English Heritage and English Nature). Anglican parish churches are already bound by state legislation in the following areas:

a) In England and Wales repairs and alterations to Anglican churches are governed by the faculty system instead of by local authority planning law. English law has now built a number of amenity societies into the faculty system so that they have a legal right to be involved in any decisions. They have the power to inflict delay and cost but are not required to contribute financially. When a congregation is attempting to upgrade its listed building for 21st century use they are faced with a mountain to climb which is not of their own making. The amenity societies are:

- The Society for the Protection of Ancient Buildings
- The Council for British Archaeology (churchyards can be key elements in any modernisation because of where any foul water drainage has to be routed)
- The Ancient Monuments Society
- The Georgian Group
- The Victorian Society
- The Twentieth Century Society

b) In England government aid for buildings is also operated through the Redundant Churches Fund. This limited fund can be used to put some old/dilapidated churches into a state where they can be mothballed. If the Church of England wants to take totally redundant buildings out of regular use, these can, if of sufficient heritage importance, be made over to the Redundant Churches Fund. However, these buildings may even then exert a negative influence upon the church's mission. This is because:

- There can be an expectation of occasional services in them "for old times' sake". Such special events consume expensive and valuable clergy time as well as inspiring a shallow nostalgia and taking the attention and time of worshippers away from the more pressing task of spreading the gospel in the world of today. The idolatry of buildings is an ever-present danger.

- These buildings are a financial burden on the diocese, which becomes responsible for future upkeep.

So serving the gospel, that the nation and its heritage may live and not die

From the point of view of those for whom preservation of our buildings heritage is a priority, it would be very convenient if the church, and particularly the Anglican wing, would co-operate in keeping all that we possess as it is, for ever, museum-style. This would never work, however. The church would die as a living body of worshippers, and the nation would slip even further into a moral, spiritual and financial pit. There would be insufficient people of goodwill around to use, care for, and protect the buildings. The finance required would dry up. Yet there would be sufficient arsonists, vandals and anti-Christian groups around to ensure the destruction of the buildings or at least of their contents, over the generation or two after the local Christians had died out. The work of the gospel and sensitive but sensible conservation actually go together. We must so serve the gospel, and make our ancient buildings serve the gospel, that the nation and its heritage may live. Where conservation law in the form of Grade I and Grade II listing of ancient churches is preventing such sensible long-term conservation, Christians nationwide should be peacefully agitating for that law to be changed.

We have already noted the teaching of Isaiah about accepting one's changed role. Another Old Testament prophet, Jeremiah, has similar teaching at Chapter 27:17. In relation to venerable church buildings the message is: "…accept the real situation. Serve in that situation and live. Why should this place become a ruin?"

Buildings can serve the gospel of God's love in Jesus Christ by being dedicated to demonstrating his love for a world in need, as well by remaining consecrated for worship of his Holy Name. Making our ancient buildings serve rather than hinder the gospel is all part of the process of updating our "business shape" referred to above in connection with the re-drawing of boundaries. The church has an eternal nature and shape, which must not be altered if it is to remain true to the Word of God, but to fail to adapt its business shape in order to faithfully serve the current shape of the world is a grave mistake. It is simply not true that the church is exempt from the business rules for reaching one's market. As already mentioned, when businesses have to slim down and regroup there is usually pain before there can be progress again. This is true for the church in these islands. The level of pain for many becomes clear as we look at what serious slimming could involve; this I have attempted to do in the next chapter. The aim of my suggestions is to promote as much conservation as will work in the long term, while in the short term kick-starting the traditional church to grow again. If the traditional church chooses not to grow again, it will die along with its buildings heritage. God will simply continue his gospel work with the new churches which do not concern themselves overmuch with what age of building they use, if any, provided they can get on with the primary work of the gospel.

To sum up

The challenge to Christians in traditional churches is:

- Are we content that gospel resources continue to be compelled to serve our heritage of church structures?

- Or are we determined that our church heritage shall serve the cause of the gospel?

CHAPTER 6   REDEVELOPMENT OF OUR CHURCH BUILDINGS

Use of historic buildings as church centres

In Chapter 4 the proposals for a successor to the parish, the "catchment", were looked at in some detail. It was evident that in the new buildings layout envisaged by the catchment system only a few of our present church buildings would be required for redevelopment as church centres. Any building that were required would need to be:

- situated in the correct strategic position – that is in or convenient to the "high street" which serves an entire catchment;

- of sufficient proportions, including its surrounding land, to provide space to welcome and accommodate the worshippers of the catchment mostly arriving by car.

Buildings not needed to form church centres

The location of a building matters in relation to the present day shape of the community. Just as a retail business pays attention to the position of premises in order to catch trade, so should the church with its buildings. The level of investment should be proportionate to the crowd levels that can be expected. Crowd levels depend on how people go about their daily life. We should not forget that this daily life includes day trips, weekend breaks and holidays. The italicised headings below are the different kinds of position on the landscape in which church buildings exist. Suggestions for re-use are given under each heading for that particular kind of site because redevelopment needs to be done according to geographical position. These suggestions incorporate the principle worked out in Chapter 5 that our heritage of buildings needs to be adapted so as to provide a living-gospel inspiration to the nation. These suggestions are primarily aimed at the Anglican part of our buildings heritage, because that is where the problem of outdated structures is most acute. However there are quite a number of buildings that are already shared in local ecumenical programmes and hopefully this trend will grow. The material offered below is not therefore to be regarded as necessarily only applicable to Anglican church buildings.

Type 1   Churches outside villages in open countryside

If it is situated on a major tourist track or waterway route, and there are sufficient Christians in the catchment to redevelop and use it for the gospel, then such church buildings should be used as welcome centres for tourists. The main nave section of the building can be used as a craft or art exhibition hall and tearoom, with the chancel separated off for prayer/counselling. This kind of use has already been started in certain tourist hot spots. Resources to make it work may have to come from a wider area than the catchment.

If both the above conditions were not met, then the building on its own would have to speak faith to the few visitors who do seek it out. In any event, it needs to be as easily maintained and inspiring as possible. This would mean giving up the struggle to maintain it as a roofed and windowed structure, which usually ends up a nasty vandalised wreck. Instead it should be reduced to a roofless ruin that is well maintained and set in grounds that are maintained by grazing. In reducing the building to manageable proportions, care should be taken to preserve any nave arches. These "vertebrae" of the building, together with the tower, are the most distinctive part of a church building. These two features usually carry the main weight of architectural heritage. As the nave arches speak most clearly of a history of worship to a person standing in the building, so the tower (and if low maintenance, a spire) speak in the same way to anyone standing at a distance away. They are the parts that would be most valuable for integration into a new church centre, if the site one day became the centrepiece of a new town.

For ease of maintenance, the floor of the retained building should be concreted to prevent rain from forming into ponds. It should be railed off to allow cattle to graze the surrounding ground. Free welcome/evangelistic leaflets could be available from a secured plastic fronted box after the style of forestry tourist locations.

Diagram 21 BASIC INSPIRING RUIN OUTSIDE A VILLAGE

1 Village - ½ mile away   3 Tower/entrance
2 Nave stripped of roof and side-aisles   4 Grounds maintenance limited to path to entrance

In some instances, churches outside villages are on much used pedestrian or motorised routes which means they lend themselves to frequent use as places of prayer and reflection. Here an enhancing feature could be a small reinforced concrete balcony with a similarly constructed part-roof. This would be at the rear of the nave to provide just enough shelter for those who want to stay to pray in bad weather. It would also help provide shelter for Christian booklets. Wall safe provision could allow for the sale of these and for donations. If there are important pieces of furniture or works of art which once adorned the building and are now on display elsewhere, details could be provided.

In the illustration below the shortest route to the church building is across the fields. This worked very well in the 12th century when the church was built and for a further seven centuries. However, while this building remains a parish church trying to provide for the spiritual needs of the village in the 21st century, the likelihood is that the great majority of church users will travel there by car along the lane which leads to the east side of the churchyard. In the present century, walking across the fields is possibly less safe than it would have been in former times.

Diagram 22 ENHANCED INSPIRING RUIN OUTSIDE A VILLAGE

1 Balcony   2 Stairs   3 Grazing   4 Village   5 Public footpath

Type 2   Churches in the centre of commuter (or large) country villages

A part of such a building should be adapted as an easily maintained substation. The rest of the structure should be developed according to the needs and situation of that village. In many cases, villages have not waited for the church to redevelop its building to provide a warm and welcoming environment for social gatherings. During the last century the village community has simply gone ahead and built or adapted a social centre fit for modern use. There may or may not be capacity in the village for more meeting space to be maintained and taken up by users such as playgroups. There may be an overriding need for affordable housing in the village, in which case that could be the right way to redevelop the bulk of the church building. Or there may be a dire need for employment/training so that this should form the centrepiece of what is done with the old church nave. The church should be in the forefront of compassion and care for all God's children. In most cases it would be wise to include at least one dwelling in the redevelopment so that the building is not isolated and unsupervised.

Diagram 23   CHURCH IN CENTRE OF A LARGE VILLAGE

1 Improved car access   2 Flat for use by key missionary workers 3 Community meeting rooms
4 Substation with separate entrance on main street   5 Peal of bells

68

Type 3   Churches central to small country villages/hamlets

The building could be redeveloped as in type 2 above if the village is resourceful enough. If not, an element of reduction of the bulk of the building to an inspiring roofless relic as in type 1 would be required. There should certainly be a substation and usable bell incorporated into the scheme. From a heating point of view, a modern prefabricated structure set within the relic would probably be more viable.

The roofless relic could be rendered more versatile by the incorporation of non-ferrous fixing points into the masonry so that a specialist contractor could canvass it over marquee-style. For particular summer occasions the building could then be used for a large gathering. Weddings might be accommodated in this way where the family concerned was prepared to pay the cost.

Diagram 24   CHURCH IN CENTRE OF A SMALL VILLAGE

1 Substation with outside seat, notice board
  and free literature panel
2 Rented housing
3 Car parking

4 Previous parish church: a well maintained ruin
5 Concourse
6 Grazing with cattle-proof barrier along south colonnade

Type 4   Churches on the edge of villages

These buildings are in many cases currently well maintained structurally. They are not however the kind of place where a substation could be effectively sited and used. Access is frequently difficult for the very young and the very old. If there is an overriding need in the locality for such a building to be developed for example as a day nursery, playgroup or youth centre and there are resources of people to make it happen and keep it running, then that would be an excellent form of re-use. There might not be any such need locally but the building could still be in demand for redevelopment and use to meet the needs of less privileged people further afield. For instance, local Christians and others of a compassionate nature might feel called to provide holidays for underprivileged people from British or East European cities. An old church building could be converted into either holiday accommodation or be adapted to provide a day centre and lunch club for those holidaymakers who were staying with local people for bed and breakfast. Careful insertion of an extra floor in the nave could provide upstairs and ground floor areas that are easier to heat and more versatile than a single high space.

Type 5   Churches in the middle of urban open spaces

These buildings can share similar access-with-safety problems as churches in open countryside or on the edge of villages. The suggestions offered for those buildings are equally valid for these.

Type 6   Churches in industrial or commercial areas and those in the middle of urban arterial roads

These buildings are a distance from residents who may live in the area or are dangerous to reach. They should be used in one of the following ways:

- They could be used for the good of the area around them or for mission to it. Examples could be a multi-storey car park, lunch club or industrial mission centre. A well-placed prayer chapel would be included within the building in each case.

- Following demolition, the land could be sold for redevelopment at a good price. This may be with a suite of offices retained as part of the deal if an office block is built on the site and if the mission of the church currently requires office space in the area.

- They should be retained as an inspiring relic as in type 1 and so provide open air sitting space for workers in their lunch hour. This has already been done in many places.

Type 7   Churches central to residential localities in towns and cities

These buildings should be treated as in type 2 above.

Type 8   Churches in, but not central to, residential localities in towns and cities

Efforts to maintain these as a place of worship for the Christian community should cease even in substation terms. They may be suitable to be sold for redevelopment as housing. They could nevertheless still be usefully redeveloped to cater for community need, either local, national, or international as in type 4. The Venerable David Lee, Archdeacon of Llandaff, wrote to the Church Times on 6 December 1996 about using such a building as a base to provide what is lacking in the area. In many urban areas it is not hard to find gaps in social provision. Some places lack resident teachers and other professionals. One scenario would therefore be for local Christians to pray for and call some Christian professionals to form a community living in a set of flats formed from an old church building. Or, if there are no Christians locally with a vocation to work along any of these lines, the building should be treated as in type 1, second and third paragraphs.

CHAPTER 7   INSIGHTS FROM FRANCE - *REAMENAGEMENT PASTORAL*

Coping with an old parish system

It is important that all the proposals in the preceding chapters be seen in a wider context. We need to take note of what is being said (and even *done*) in other places beyond England and Wales. In Chapter 2 the teaching of the Scottish report, *Church without Walls,* was quoted to highlight the failure of the church to "go with the gospel" from a parish context. When we look southwards from England and Wales we find also that the French Catholic Church has much to say on this same problem.

The French Catholic Church is the body still linked to the country's ancient parish churches. It faces a challenge parallel to, but not the same as, the Anglican Church in England and Wales.

During a large part of the 20th century certain French theologians and bishops produced teaching on re-shaping the church for modern mission far more perceptive than any found in the UK during the same period. When the author visited three northern French dioceses in 1996 he was privileged to be present while some of this teaching was being imparted to clergy and laity; in the Nancy et Toul Diocese the Bishop had produced a second edition of his *Collaborer pour la Mission.* By 1996 a lack of priests was forcing pastoral change in a way that has not happened in the Anglican church. However the attempt was still being made in places to get round all the villages to lead eucharistic worship. Generally there did not yet seem to be the necessary wholesale shift in missionary method in France any more than is the case in the UK. In the present century there are some signs of giving up efforts to maintain the liturgy in French villages, whilst making the liturgy in the nearest town affirm the individuality of the various component villages in the new larger parish. Since 1905 the Catholic Church has not owned the parish churches except for a small part of the northeast. Because of this it may be in a stronger position to "walk away" from a building than is the Church of England.

Another advantage the French Catholic Church has is the historical attitude there to parish boundaries. They have not had such a rigid system whereby the parish priest is the "owner" of a territory in which he has exclusive rights to minister apart from the episcopal ministry of the bishop, as has been the case in the Anglican parish system. There have been more communities of monks and nuns with a trans-parochial ministry in a given area. Also in the 20th century organisations like JOC (outreach to young workers) have routinely operated across parish boundaries. The authority of bishops to move clergy about at will has also made for easier change because parish priests have not had the right to refuse to move. The Anglican bishops have struggled to change the pastoral map when parish clergy instituted as vicars or rectors have the freehold and do not therefore have to move until retirement (though the freehold may prove a useful safeguard where Anglican dioceses try to "dump" too many ailing structures on a single priest). Although a lack of priests must be difficult to cope with in the short term, it may result in new healthy structures being put in place all the sooner, provided enough laity can be motivated and matured in time to make them work.

Diagram 25   A TYPE OF SUBSTATION IN THE DIOCESE OF BEAUVAIS – AD 1996

The above illustration is from a photograph that the author took after inspecting the interior of the parish church in a French village. A buttress of this building appears on the right hand side of the picture. The arch in the centre background would originally have allowed wheeled access to the rear of the property. Before the Catholic Church bought it, the premises served as a bank. The church converted it to a "maison paroissiale" (parish house) for use as a contact point for pastoral needs, baptism and wedding enquiries. The place was effectively a small lock-up shop. The bishop licensed a layperson for a year at a time to staff this substation for the group of villages in the area. The parish church, although owned and supposedly maintained by the state, was too damp and dismal for this purpose.

The work of Canon Fernand Boulard

The references that follow are to Michael Jackson's 1960 translation of Canon Boulard's book *Premiers Itinéraires en Sociologie Religieuse,* titled *An Introduction to Religious Sociology*[41]

Each of the ten paragraphs below picks out a key point made by Canon Boulard.

a) He emphasises the importance of a missionary policy towards "wholes", ie towards each social milieu (p83).

b) He points out how effective St Paul was in his missionary strategy, and says how "his main concern was to plant the church in the great centres of influence, knowing that the rest would follow". He supports this view by quoting Cardinal Lercaro, Archbishop of Bologna, (p76) who held the first religious sociology congress in Italy in 1954.

Cardinal Lercaro had on that occasion given several New Testament examples of embryonic religious sociology in action for the Kingdom of God (pp102-103).

c) He follows up the research into the effect industry has on the church's hold on an area, when carried on according to the "money above men" principle of liberal capitalism. He concludes that we "are faced with a *conflict of civilisations*". The church's task he says is none other than "to penetrate to the core" the advancing industrial civilisation "with the Spirit of Christ" (pp16-17).

d) He emphasises the importance of Christian faith, taking note that God is not just Lord of the supernatural order but also of the natural order (p80). He goes on to call for both humble self-examination with regard to the causes of missionary failure, and confession of our own and the church's failure to pray (pp81-82).

e) He explains his concept of the *zone humaine* (translated by Jackson "natural grouping"*)*. In order to do this he focuses particularly on the Diocese of Aix-en-Provence. The Etang de Berre, north west of Marseilles, was formerly an area around a salt lagoon used by a few fishermen. It changed after the First World War, becoming a great international centre for modern industry (petrol refinery, aircraft factory etc). People came to work there from all over the world. The church in this area existed in four deaneries. As single deaneries of clergy meeting together, the church leadership would never have been geared up to confront the challenges that this new *zone humaine* presented in terms of effective mission. However, meeting together as a group of four deaneries would spark a wholly relevant agenda. As well as this *zone humaine* based upon very new and large industry, Boulard identifies other *zones* in the Diocese including a neighbouring one for agricultural workers of which the town of Salon was the centre (pp93-103).

f) Boulard estimates that "an urban area of 25,000-40,000 inhabitants generally constitutes a natural grouping (*zone humaine)* on its own" (pp98-100).

g) He says "there are marked differences in mentality within regions from one locality to another...but to the traveller it is even more clear that there is a regional tonality embracing all these obvious differences" (p93).

h) He speaks of the need for working parties and sociological research units before missions are undertaken in natural groupings/regions. He believed these would generally have to be set up for areas bigger than a single diocese because of lack of money and trained personnel (p100-102).

i) He pleads for the church to have a sociological research unit because "no one man (bishop) can have a sufficiently intimate knowledge of our complex society" (p102). Given the current rate of change in society, he would doubtless have wanted to make this point even more strongly today.

j) He calls for monasteries to become "centres of theological thinking and spiritual culture with the particular problems of the natural grouping in view" where people can come and reflect and pray about the issues. He envisaged such religious houses taking an active part in the church's work in the natural groupings in their area (pp96-97).

CHAPTER 8   THE WAY FORWARD

A – While the present age continues so must restructuring

The church in Western Europe has a lot of catching up to do in its attitude to the world God has created. In the first place we need to face up to the fact that God's creation is a developing one, especially the human part of it. We could say that many in western European churches need a crash course in creation theology. When we look to restructure the church so that we are up to date with our missionary shape, we must never think that we have arrived. If we do, we will simply find that the creation we are seeking to serve has moved on again while our backs have been turned. The following headings illustrate how fast everything is moving.

The age of the media and the global village

The global village has been more and more part of our way of life since about 1990. The September 11 terrorist outrage in New York unfolded slowly enough to be watched by millions as it was actually happening. In the business world more and more people find they have to think globally in order to survive. It is hard to see exactly how the church's structure needs to adapt in order to relate, except that it clearly needs international ears and an international voice. The Roman Catholic Church has the most international tradition of all Christian bodies and it has the most audible centralised mouthpiece in the form of the Vatican and a pope. Non-Roman Catholic churches have their own international structures and there is also their combined forum, the World Council of Churches. Access to the media remains the key to effectiveness for any international mouthpiece of the church as it does for a national or regional mouthpiece. Resources need to be made available within the church at whatever level to enable good input to the media. If the media decides it is going to suppress the Christian viewpoint as offered to it, the church is right to use a "plan B". Plan B is simply to ensure a hearing in the media by organising something the media cannot ignore – a public demonstration. Peaceful mass witness or demonstration or protest is used in the secular scene. It has proved its worth in the Christian scene and in a sense it provides an even more effective mouthpiece that the use of a prominent church leader acting alone. The peaceful mass demonstration has of course been used by Christ himself[42] and throughout Christian history. A famous third century example was the parade of the poor of Ancient Rome that led to the martyrdom of St Laurence[43] (see later in this chapter).

Too much church energy can easily go into yearly or periodic parades that the community around enjoys as a quaint custom but through which that community remains unchallenged. There is a need for a good number of demonstrations to be of a one-off or spur-of-the-moment nature. Congregations need to be taught that peaceful mass witness or demonstration should be an extension of the church's structure. The communication of issues about which there needs to be some specific witness requires the right means of communication and feedback within congregations. The best means of this is through use of a cell church structure.

Edge or out-of-town shopping malls

These have had the effect of diminishing the traditional high street in certain areas. However, they are unlikely to annihilate the high street or town centre, particularly where there are market stalls, good parking and other attractions in old town centres. Where large out-of-town facilities exist, they are likely to serve a wider area than the catchment centred on the nearest town. Examples are the out-of-town shopping facilities around Calais and Dover. These not only cater for Pas de Calais and Kent east of Canterbury but for the international travelling public. As such, they need the same outreach structure within them as I have recommended for motorway service areas.

Telephone banking, internet shopping and office-working from home

High street visits by customers for banking and shopping will be reduced by the use of their telephone lines to make transactions of various types. Paying in cheques and certain cash withdrawals still need high street visits. However, reduction in time spent in an office workplace could increase time spent within one's nearest town because travel to work in a distant city becomes unnecessary every working day.

International commuting to work

Across Europe there are businesses that are staffed by an international workforce who travel back to their respective homelands either every weekend or at less frequent intervals. Some of these businesses operate in the great urban and commercial cities of Europe; others are remote such as North Sea oilrigs. This is a new phenomenon. Less than twenty years ago international companies brought many native English speakers to live with their families in mainland Europe because they needed their workers to speak and write well in English. Now, particularly in the European Union, English is so well taught in school and is so available on television channels, that it is no longer necessary to tempt workers to move over from the British Isles or North America with a good resettlement package for the whole family. It is cheaper to employ indigenous workers locally.

This means that UK residents who want to work in mainland Europe retain their home in the UK and travel by air to stay for four or five nights wherever they have a job. These jobs are often contracts of around one year but may be replaced by a similar post in the same or another EU country. The life is therefore stressful and also lonely midweek. The time workers spend in their "work country" is similar in any one week to that which seafarers would spend half a century ago in a European port and equivalent to that spent by seafarers today when there is a little repair work needed on their ship. With containerisation and quick turn-round tanker terminals, unloading of ships now tends to take only hours rather than days.

In the late 20th century in the Port of Rotterdam the Christian ministry to seafarers had a hard time to keep up with the increasing volume of work as well as with changes in cargo handling patterns. At that time the different denominations worked the port as one team in order to cope with the demands of the situation. The need for similar co-operation in mission is clear in the matter of reaching international commuters. There should be good contacts through airports and airlines, good outreach company by company, and well-placed pastoral groups midweek. Each national church in Europe needs to have sympathetic follow-up arrangements to link care for their nationals at home with any united ministry that is achieved in the workplace. In short, industrial mission needs to be more than national. It needs to be Europe-wide.

Restructuring the church has to be continuous for a society which is always moving on. Note the plea of Canon Boulard for a sociological research unit for the church.[44]

B – Practical steps leading to restructuring

Far from wanting to face and respond to the great social changes surrounding the church, many members of congregations are loath to accept the smallest of changes to the way things are done in their church. There are some however who have a burden for seeing the gospel at work in the community and who can clearly see that many traditions are being used to obstruct outreach. They are ready for structural change. Just as Jesus did, we also need to look for where the Father is already at work and do our part there.[45]

Therefore we need Christian gatherings of those who *want* to see the church correctly structured. Many realise that it is far from properly structured the way it is. They may, however, currently lack teaching on biblical principles of mission and on how to sift and reinterpret what is of value in church tradition. These gatherings need to happen locally, nationally and internationally. They could be either single or multi-denominational. At these there should be:

Sustained teaching on what verses such as Mark 16:15 mean in practice today
This would include sharing good news of best practice where this is already happening in other churches or nations (compare St Paul's use of one nation/church to spur on one another as in 2 Corinthians 8:1-8 and Romans 11:13-14, and see above Chapter 7, final paragraph). Some teaching material is offered in Section C.

Repentance for the church's slumber and idolatry of the institution
According to the Bible we can and should repent on behalf of our community as well as on our own individual account. For many who are weary of trying to maintain the parts of church structure that are near collapse, such repentance could be a joyful enterprise. This weariness in the present century has produced a lack of lay people willing to stand for office in local churches. Is not this proof enough that the structure is struggling?

Ministry in the Spirit and prayer for the coming of the Holy Spirit
We need intercession, fasting and ministry to open the door to the Holy Spirit. We need him to set free imprisoned minds, and to reveal Christ and his Word to church members and to those searching for the meaning of life. We should test, take to heart, and pray through any prophetic words which the Spirit wants the European churches to hear today. An example of this is the prophecy of 1998 referred to on page 85. The disease affecting the churches of Western Europe is far too virulent to be overcome by a simple call to

become missionary again. It is a spiritual problem and New Testament spiritual weapons are needed to overcome it (see 2 Corinthians 10:3-5 and Ephesians 6:10-18).

Prayer and action for specific projects

There needs to be prayer and the offer of prophetic encouragement and guidance wherever there are efforts being made to move the churches from a maintenance culture to a missionary one. Support should be given to both local and national projects. In particular, inter-church gospel outreach within present day social structures should be a priority for prayer and action. Likewise, prayer and support is needed for the coming together of church lawyers from the different traditions in order to discern ways through the legal constraints that hinder the change from maintenance to mission. The churches need to present a united front if they are to get the lawmakers of Parliament and the nation as a whole to hear them.

C – Material for teaching groups, congregations and gatherings

Old and New Testaments

Luke & Hebrews

The church in Europe has a great need to escape the clutches of that which is passing away. In Luke 21 people draw Jesus' attention to the fine heritage of Temple buildings. He proceeds to teach on the subject of the approaching end of the era of the Jerusalem Temple, as well as the end of this age when he will come again in glory. The letter to the Hebrews may have been written shortly after AD 60 to warn Hebrew Christians living near the Jerusalem Temple not to be focused on the building and its ongoing Old Testament priestly ritual, but to rely wholly on the finished priestly work of Christ. They needed to be free to flee in good time before the siege of Jerusalem began in AD 68. This led to the destruction of the city and its Temple two years later. "Keep awake then and watch at all times, praying that you may have the full strength *and* ability *and* be accounted worthy to escape all these things that will take place" (AMP). The fall of Jerusalem might be likened to the fall of the medieval church structure. We should not cling to something which although obsolete has the power to drag us down with it. If we are truly a people who are awake and watching and praying, we will not want to cling to what is obsolete, but will rather be focused on the living Lord Jesus Christ and his gospel business for today.

Jeremiah 7 (as on front cover)

"Do not trust in these deceptive words: 'This is the temple of the Lord, the temple of the Lord, the temple of the Lord'" (Jeremiah 7:4, RSV); "I gave your ancestors no commands about burnt offerings or any other kinds of sacrifices, when I brought them out of Egypt. But this command I gave them, 'Obey my voice…'"(Jeremiah 7:22-26, GNT). Note especially "went backward and not forward" (Jeremiah 7:24, RSV). These texts show how God has had to warn his people in the past about the dangers of trusting in the establishment of a sacred building rather than in him, and of thinking that "chalking up" a lot of liturgical services is necessarily a way of listening, prayerfully obeying and moving along with God on his appointed path. If our attention is not upon the Lord, we will miss his call to go forward.

Haggai

To make a market work the customers have to exist in sufficient numbers. That means there is a point when customer numbers rise to a critical mass of people which is capable of making the market viable. So many of our congregations are too small for the big-time worship they attempt Sunday by Sunday. They do not consist of the critical mass needed for large-scale worship celebrations. How can it be Christian to refuse to gather in a critical mass/market town for a full celebration of our worship when we shop for the wellbeing of our own households in a critical mass? Compare the words of Haggai 1:4, "My people, why should you be living in well-built houses while my house lies in ruins?" (GNT)

Revelation

Our God is in the business of makings things new (Revelation 21:5, but compare the Anglican Collect for Epiphany 2 in Common Worship where it is our lives he wants to make new). "Be zealous and repent" (Revelation 3:19 (RSV) and compare Revelation 2:5, 16-17, 3:3, 13 and 22). Spiritual gold, clothes and vision are available on the Lord's terms (Revelation 3:18).

Acts

In the speech of St Stephen in Acts 7 he quotes Isaiah 66:1-2. His accusers exhibit much touchiness about their building. Perhaps they rather idolise the Temple. By contrast it was the temple/body of Christ whose welfare Stephen had been appointed to oversee. See Jeremiah 11:16 with regard to the point made in the chapter on gospel and heritage that mere preservation of ancient churches will result in their destruction. This text speaks of God having once acknowledged his people as a green, beautiful and fruitful olive tree, but now with a roar of a great tempest he will set fire to this tree and its branches will be consumed. The reason for this is found in the next verse: idolatry. Jeremiah in 7:14 and 26:6-9 give warning of the "Shiloh treatment" that is looming over unfaithful Israel's Temple, a temple in which they have wrongly trusted.

Deuteronomy

Deut 9:23 refers to Kadeshbarnea. We hear of Israel's refusal to go up and take the land. Compare the refusal of the church to move into the modern world with the gospel.

3 John

Compare Gaius, who is loyal to the truth and a supporter of catholic provision of prophecy from other parts of the worldwide church, with Diotrephes. Diotrephes is a party political parochial empire builder. This man refuses apostolic authority and prophetic authority which is provided to confirm God's will for a local church. Note that "the household of God" is "built upon the foundation of the apostles and prophets" (Ephesians 2:20).

2 Corinthians

In 2 Corinthians 4:5 Paul says, "For what we preach is not ourselves but Jesus Christ as Lord..." (RSV). Compare the church when it worships and preaches itself and is therefore heading for emptiness and bankruptcy.

2 Kings

In 2 Kings 23 King Josiah reforms corrupt structures but not men's hearts. Wrong ways were reinstated after his death. There needed to be the "death" of the nation through exile in Babylon to curb its idolatry; ultimately this disease is only cured through the grace of Jesus Christ crucified and risen. We may compare the treatment needed today where there is idolatry in the church.

Matthew

Matt 5:14 speaks of "a city set on a hill". We are to affirm and exemplify creation before men. What a tragedy that we put the light of Christ inside an antique "tub". We water down/leach the salt which we should make freely available to give savour to life today. Christ centred worship is beautiful and attractive to those who are seeking the truth – Matthew 26:6-13.

Mark

Our buildings and parish heritage, worshipped for themselves, are delightful but deceitful riches (Mark 4:19). As in the Parable of the Sower (4:3-9) they are choking the gospel seed that is proving unfruitful.

Everyday life

Successive UK governments have lacked rigour for updating the transport system and communities are being throttled as a result. Compare the church's lack of rigour with its outdated structures and its "gasping for life and forward movement".

The church is like a fishing fleet that is old and mothballed and in port rather than refitted and out catching fish. It needs refitting to be able to stand the storms of post-modern materialism. Part of this refitting is the retraining of its leaders to demonstrate tough love in effecting necessary change while riding out the storms of protest that will result, however loving they have tried to be.

Pruning personnel needs very thick gloves. In John 15 Jesus used the picture of a vine that needed pruning to be fruitful to teach his disciples how they would bear fruit for his Kingdom. The principles of pruning are:

a) Look at the bush or tree and imagine it as the correct shape for producing the maximum amount of flower or fruit. For this to happen the branches will need to be as short as possible so that energy is not wasted in bringing nourishment from the roots to the fruit buds. The fruit spurs and buds need to have the maximum exposure to sunshine and to air (so as not to be damaged by chafing each other[46]).

b) Decide which bits of the existing woodwork are to be retained as part of the scheme envisaged in a).

c) Remove the rest of the growth which will in fact be either rank and leggy producing only or mostly leaves, diseased, spindly and stunted, dying or dead.

d) Make the cuts with care with a sharp implement to minimise bleeding and the entry of disease. If desirable, cover the cut surfaces to keep out the elements and disease.

e) Wait for God's gift of growth. The bush or tree will need to fill the appointed airspace and become its full fruit-bearing shape. In the case of fruit trees this can take a few seasons.

What the western European church needs is to have its unproductive bits lovingly removed in order to make space for a new and productive structure that occupies all the airspaces of the modern world where God wants to do business. Like Mary, we are to be the handmaid of the Lord, pregnant and nimble at the same time (Luke 1:36-56). Currently we are more like an overweight and unproductive pensioner. The clergy and those who work alongside them cannot, and should not, continue to cope with the rank growth of centuries, *and* be expected to produce fruit in the modern European world.

What we are currently busy trying to add on to traditional shape of the Church of England needs to be seen in the context of pruning for fruitfulness. Church plants doubtless have their place in big impersonal environments like inner London; souls are being saved through their existence. Fresh Expressions of church often rely on the existing struggling parish system to maintain them and are very hard work if an incumbent has to keep fulfilling all the legal requirements of the job at the same time. They are needed, but if they remain as an add-on for too many years rather than new growth *replacing* old, they will simply worsen an already alarming rate of clergy burnout. In the long term we need to confront the "choice culture" and get ourselves a tidy fruit-producing tree rather than one which is trying to cater for every kind of preference at parish level. Catchments at least would provide a bigger base from which to connect with the need for all styles of worship.

First and Second World Wars

On the subject of strategy

To take an analogy from the First World War, the church's foot-soldiers are being pointlessly slaughtered because old generals are still fighting yesterday's war. Montgomery saw this First World War slaughter for what it was. By the Second World War he had studied and produced updated strategy that did not waste human resources.[47] Monty enjoined "Courage, integrity and enthusiasm"[48] and practised these things himself both before and during the war. During the Second World War handheld anti-tank weapons were developed. This meant that on open ground tanks could no longer dominate infantry. The church needs to become expert at picking off the heavy armour of secularism by the use of small groups fighting with prayer.

When the professionals are not allowed to be strategists their professionalism is squandered

In early summer 1941 Hitler sent the German Army to invade the Soviet Union. His army made fast progress, but in the event not quite fast enough. When winter struck they were still just outside Moscow. Unlike the Russians, they were not equipped for severe winter weather and should have withdrawn to nearby towns for shelter. Hitler however regarded every square yard of his Third Reich as non-negotiable and would not allow this. His troops suffered terribly from the weather and from counter attack by the Russians. This unrealistic attitude and strategic interference by Hitler helped him to lose the war.[49]

A similar attitude will lose the church its "war" if it insists on holding on to its whole panoply of parish churches in their under-resourced and often frigid state. In the early 2000s an actual case occurred of a keen 92 year old Anglican churchgoer who attended his rural parish church in midwinter. Unfortunately his worsening circulation wasn't up to the challenge of the under-resourced church heating. When he got home after the service his faculties needed quite a time to thaw out before he could even recognise his wife. At the other end of the age range we "freeze out" people who, as Rev Bob Hopper pointed out,[50] will not put up with 18th century facilities in the 21st century.

Professionalism is a vital ingredient, indeed one of God's gifts, for winning a campaign

Dowding, the Second World War Air Force leader, had a "deep understanding of technology" wrote Stephen Bungay in The Times.[51] Dowding had prepared the aerial defence of London before the Second World War began. The courage of "The Few" (fighter pilots in the Battle of Britain) was great but it was well directed.[52] Compare the more tragic courage of First World War infantry on both sides.

About the need for prayer as a body

After the fall of France in 1940 Britain was lacking the necessary fully-equipped land forces to resist an invasion if one had come. We did however have some fighter aircraft, and radar masts were already in position on the relevant parts of our coastline. Therefore the Battle of Britain was won – just, because our fighter aircraft were guided quickly and accurately by radar to precisely where they were needed. The use of radar is a picture of the church listening to God and praying so that it positions itself more and more where it can have an impact for the Kingdom of God, and where its effort can bear fruit. We should be like Jesus: at work where the Father (John 5:19) is at work, not in some other place that happens to take our fancy. As a church we must never neglect to use prayer – our most vital weapon.

About the need for good communication to the nation

The Mulberry harbours, towed across the Channel in 1944, were an important part of the invasion of Normandy. They provided port facilities to supply the invasion forces while

French ports were still in enemy hands. If the use of media channels is denied to the churches they should construct their own. TV, radio and the press are like ports of entry to reach the nation. The saying that the "real work" of the church is done in the parishes needs to be challenged with the truth that the work of the gospel needs to be vigorously pursued at all levels – locally, city-wide, regionally, nationally and internationally.

International church ministry

Compare the good co-operation between European churches to provide a ministry for the international seafaring community in its need, with the virtual non-provision of ministry to the international commuting community in its need.

We need an association of European churches to work at this. Paul in Acts 28:30 was available to "all who came to him" (RSV) in Rome including Jews in verse 17. After the expulsion of Jews by the Emperor Claudius in Acts 18, there were clearly Jews in Rome again. So there was plenty of migration and movement of people in New Testament times. The gospel for Europe is trapped in medieval wineskins made worse by the church splits of the last millennium.

Church history

In the third century, during state persecution under the Roman Empire, the church at Rome was given a deadline by which it had to hand over its precious possessions. The martyrdom of Laurence, one of the Pope's deacons, occurred when he enriched the poor of Rome with the church's treasure and then presented them to the imperial authorities as the church's real treasure. The authorities were not amused; Laurence was executed.[53] What is our treasure today? Is it our parochial inheritance, or the poor whom we could use some of that inheritance to bless? See suggested use of churches in location type 4 in Chapter 6.

Under the communist regime in East Germany, the Lutheran Bishop of Leipzig was persecuted by the authorities. Their tactic was to seek to keep him at his desk so that he could not function as an effective leader and pastor. They set out to neutralise him with piles of paperwork which they required in order that he function within the law. Today British law so clogs up the development, modernisation and use of the inheritance of parishes and old church buildings, that we effectively have persecution of the church. The nation and Parliament may not realise this but they need to be alerted to what is being done in their name to constrict the ability of the church to serve the people.[54]

In 1998 John Mulinde of World Trumpet Mission, Uganda,[55] spoke a prophetic warning to Europe in relation to the spiritual darkness spreading across our nations. But along with this was a word of encouragement to Christians of all denominations to turn back to God in prayer for revival. This call was particularly aimed at Britain, but also at France and included a bible text: Isaiah 60:1-5.

CONCLUSION

Death is an option for the church in Western Europe. There have been parts of the world where the church has been in existence for quite a long time and then has been extinguished. The Roman province of Africa, centred on what is now Tunisia, is such a place.

The paragraph above headed *Deuteronomy* is included as an example of God's people refusing to believe in his power to go before them. Through lack of faith they disobey his call to move into the land allocated to them. The problem in today's western European church is similar in that our faith in God is patchy and shaky. It is also adulterated with a heavy dose of idolatry as this book has been at pains to point out. The delay in going in to take the land described in Deuteronomy 9 lasted 40 years and involved the judgement of God in the form of serious loss of numbers. The historic churches in this part of the world have had plenty of teaching[56] about restructuring for 40 years now and have done very little about it. In that period they have suffered a serious loss of numbers. Their nations have steadily lost their spiritual and moral life.

The business of the book of Deuteronomy as a whole is to challenge God's people in their settled prosperous state. Prosperity always carries a greater danger of idolatry because we are the more tempted to think we can manage without God. Deuteronomy is all about applying the "wilderness faith" to a settled Israel. In the time of Moses, when Israel wandered between Egypt and Canaan, the people had to depend on God for physical survival. In Deuteronomy 30:15-20 the passage shows Moses putting yet again before the people the choice of blessing or curse, life or death. There is *blessing* in following the path of faithfulness, and *curse* in following the path of idolatry. Idolatry is the people's worst sin then, as now. This is because it is a rejection of God in favour of something or someone we consider more important. Such rejection, if persisted in, ends in death. The Deuteronomy 30 passage says,

> "But if your heart turns away, and you will not hear, but are drawn away to worship other gods and serve them, I declare to you this day, that you shall perish…" (RSV)

> "I call heaven and earth to witness against you this day: I set before you life or death, blessing or curse. Choose life, so that you and your descendants may live, loving your God, obeying his voice, clinging to him…" (RSV)

Though we now live in the Christian era, this Deuteronomy message still applies to us.

NOTES

INTRODUCTION
[1] Boulard, F (1954) *Premiers Itinéraires en Sociologie Religieuse,* Paris, Les Editions Ouvrières
[2] Boulard, F, translated by Jackson, MJ (1960*) An Introduction To Religious Sociology: Pioneer Work In France,* London, Darton, Longman and Todd
[3] See 1 John 4:19-21

CHAPTER 1
[4] See Chapter 7 paragraph b) p74
[5] Adapted map from *The Oxford Illustrated Encyclopedia* (OUP, 2005), copyright © Oxford University Press 1998, reprinted by permission of Oxford University Press
[6] See start of Chapter 2 p25
[7] Lean, G (1964) *John Wesley, Anglican*, London, Blandford, pp41-42
Wesley, J (1891) *Wesley His Own Biographer*, London, CH Kelly, pp104-106

CHAPTER 2
[8] According to Bagster's *Analytical Greek Lexicon*, Samuel Bagster & Sons Ltd, p239, the Greek word for creation here actually focuses on the human creation
[9] See Chapter 7 paragraphs c) and d) p75
[10] See Chapter 7 paragraph d) p75
[11] The Industrial Mission Association, through IMA Agenda editor, Rev Stephen Hazlett, an Industrial Chaplain in Sunderland and member of the National Executive Committee
[12] The Church of Scotland (2001) *Church Without Walls: Report to the General Assembly*
[13] The idea of life zone is built up from what an individual nuclear family does with its time, ie where it fully lives. The French term *zone humaine*, which we owe to Boulard, was an inspiration. Here life zone, though meaning something slightly different to *zone humaine,* is a concept very much in sympathy with it. Once the church has responded to the existence of life zones, it needs to do mission within each *zone humaine* found within a life zone. See Chapter 7 paragraph e) p75
[14] See Chapter 7 paragraph f) p75
[15] See Chapter 7 paragraph g) p75
[16] This is not as dire as in France where it can get as bad as 1/43. Sadly the Church of England seems often to start the process of restructuring by linking immediately adjoining parishes to a market town, while neglecting to properly incorporate the country parishes which are a little further out, but still dependent, in natural creation terms, on that town. The "leftover" parishes then end up as long "strings" under a priest-in-charge on the circumference. He or she is then left to minister in six or more units that have little that they share in common apart having links to a town from which they are pastorally separated.
[17] See also Chapter 7 paragraph c) p75
[18] Note an example which occurred on Channel 4, *The Real Jesus Christ* programme of 20 December 2000 dealing with the person of Christ with professors going on at length about the Dead Sea Scrolls, John the Baptist, and the early Jerusalem Church version versus St Paul's version and which won. In my opinion, the programme only half-quoted the words

of Peter in Matthew 16:16 "You are the Christ" ie omitting "the Son of the living God". (RSV) See Jeremiah 16:19

[19] See Chapter 7 paragraph h) p75

CHAPTER 3

[20] The current name of Ripon Diocese is Ripon and Leeds

[21] Information from *Crockford's Clerical Directory*, London, Church House Publishing. Copyright © The Archbishops' Council (1995). Used by kind permission

[22] Adapted from www.bbc.co.uk and www.bbc.co.uk/wales

[23] From www.communities.gov.uk. Reproduced under the terms of the Click-Use Licence

[24] Used by permission of The Catholic Bishops' Conference of England and Wales, www.catholic-ew.org.uk

[25] © Trustees for Methodist Church Purposes. Used by kind permission of The Methodist Publishing House. www.mph.org.uk

[26] Used by permission of the Baptist Union of Great Britain, www.baptist.org.uk

[27] Used by permission of the United Reformed Church

[28] Adapted from The Archbishops' Council (1995) op cit

[29] With thanks for information supplied by the Assemblies of God, www.aog.org.uk

[30] See under "Type 6 Churches in industrial or commercial areas etc" on page 70

[31] With acknowledgement to Davies, ET (1962) *The Story of the Church in Glamorgan 560-1960*, London, SPCK

CHAPTER 4

[32] See John 12:37-50 especially verse 42 and Romans 10:8-15

[33] Compare Luke 4:22-23

[34] For further information see: Montgomery, Bernard Law (1958) *The Memoirs of Field Marshal the Viscount Montgomery of Alamein*, London, Collins; Montgomery, Bernard Law (1970), *A History of Warfare*, New Edition, Jane's Publishing Co Ltd, London

[35] See Ephesians 6:12

[36] See Chapter 2 *The Two Winged Church* in Beckham, William A (1995) *The Second Reformation - Reshaping the Church for the 21st Century,* Houston, Touch Publications

[37] Hebrews 12:1

[38] See Luke 16:13 and Matthew 6:24

CHAPTER 5

[39] Extracts from *Collaborer pour la Mission* here and in Chapter 7, used by permission of the Diocese of Nancy et Toul

[40] See Chapter 7

CHAPTER 7

[41] Boulard, F, translated by Jackson, MJ (1960) *An Introduction To Religious Sociology: Pioneer Work In France,* London, Darton, Longman and Todd. Used by permission

CHAPTER 8

[42] See Matthew 21

[43] See Cross, FL (ed) (1958) *Oxford Dictionary of the Christian Church*, Oxford University Press

[44] Chapter 7 paragraph i)

[45] See John 5:19-20

[46] This may be seen as illustrative of the current problem detailed on page 27 where churches over-provide for wedding and funeral "customers", and on page 38 where they compete for a Sunday congregation.

[47] Montgomery, Bernard Law (1958) op cit pp36-37

[48] As remembered by the author when Montgomery addressed his Cadet Corps in the mid 1950s

[49] See Matanle, I (1989), *World War II,* Godalming, Surrey, CLB Publishing, pp100-104

[50] A letter published in the Church Times, 8 February 2002

[51] Bungay, S (2000), Analysis, *The Myth of "The Few" that does not add up,* The Times 2, 12 July 2000

[52] Bungay, S (2000), *The Most Dangerous Enemy: A History of the Battle of Britain,* London, Aurum Press

[53] Cross, FL (ed) (1958) op cit p790

[54] See also on page 80 in section B, last paragraph on united action to discern ways through the legal constraints

[55] www.worldtrumpetmission.org

[56] An early Church of England example was Paul, L (1964) *The Deployment and Payment of the Clergy,* London, Church Information Office